Is
Jesus
God?

Is Jesus God?

Finding Our Faith

MICHAEL MORWOOD

A Crossroad Book
The Crossroad Publishing Company
New York

The Crossroad Publishing Company
481 Eighth Avenue, New York, NY 10001

Printed in the United States of America

Library of Congress Cataloging-in-Publication Data

Morwood, Michael.
   Is Jesus God? : finding our faith / by Michael Morwood.
     p. cm.
   Includes bibliographical references.
   ISBN 0-8245-1891-8 (alk. paper)
   1. Jesus Christ – Divinity. I. Title.
BT216.3 .M67 2001
232'.8 – dc21
                                      00-012515

2   3   4   5   6   7   8   9   10   06   05   04   03   02   01

Contents

Introduction

MANY CHRISTIANS will identify dwindling, aging congregations with fewer clergy as the most challenging issues in the church today. However, the greatest challenge is far more foundational than these issues. It is the challenge of engaging basic Christian theological questions with contemporary knowledge and information. Did the first human beings cause a major disruption to their relationship with God? Did God want Jesus to die in order for humankind to be redeemed? Is Jesus God? Is God really three persons in one? It is inevitable that at the beginning of the third Christian millennium we will shape some of our responses to these questions differently from Christians of the first Christian millennium. The consequences of engaging these questions and shaping our answers now with new, contemporary knowledge and information underpin the beginning of a shift in Christian thinking that will dwarf any other shift in Christian thinking and practice in the past two thousand years.

I want this book to continue the conversation begun on these questions in *Tomorrow's Catholic: Understanding God and Jesus in a New Millennium.** Both the positive and negative reactions to *Tomorrow's Catholic* have deepened my conviction about the urgency for Christians of all denominations to engage radical questions confronting Christian faith.

---

*Melbourne: Spectrum, and Mystic, Conn.: Twenty-Third Publications, 1997.

The most central of these questions concern the identity and role of Jesus of Nazareth.

Traditional Christian theology expresses the belief that Jesus is the incarnation of the Second Person of the Blessed Trinity. Often, popular language simply says: Jesus is God. I believe the time has come to re-form Christian thinking by shifting from the belief that Jesus is essentially an incarnate god-figure on whom our access to eternal life with God depends. Far from undermining the very foundation of the Christian religion, this shift, I believe, would lead us to a better appreciation of the preaching and insights of Jesus and the message of Pentecost. I also believe there is an urgent need to have in place a well-articulated Christian spirituality in the face of the inevitable collapse of a theological system of belief dependent on Jesus being a special incarnation of God for us to be "saved."

For many Christians the questioning will seem at first hearing to be totally subversive of the foundations of Christian faith. Some will be affronted by the very fact questions are raised concerning established and clear Christian doctrine. Some will choose not to participate in any conversation and discussion about what are to them issues beyond question. However, the questions will not go away, and in fact there are many Christians who welcome the opportunity to explore reasons for believing or not believing that Jesus is God incarnate. And in today's society it is not enough just to quote authoritative sources such as Scripture, Tradition, Creeds, and official church teaching as if all discussion ends there. If Jesus is God incarnate, then let us engage the task of expressing this belief in language and ideas that correspond with today's understanding of the beginnings of the universe, the formation of planets, the emergence of life, the development of human life, and the development of culture.

I suspect that the underlying fear of open discussion is not so much the questioning itself, but rather the consequences of coming to believe that Jesus is not God incarnate. There would be major consequences for our images and language about God and redemption, church authority and its exercise of power, liturgy and our understanding of Christianity in relationship with other world religions. On the other hand, our day-to-day commitment to living as Jesus taught us to live might not change in any dramatic way.

My guess is that many readers of this book will not have engaged in discussion about whether Jesus is God. It is not the sort of topic one sees promoted on church billboards for public discussion. I suspect, however, that the next ten years will bring more and more open discussion of this issue. I predict that in this new century many committed Christians will wonder how Christianity could have stayed embedded so long in the idea that Jesus had to be interpreted as a god-figure who came down to earth to redress a terrible mistake made by the first human beings. Increasing disenchantment with institutional church structures and liturgy reliant on an outdated theological framework is inevitable.

In the past three years it has become increasingly clear to me that a central issue in the current debate about the identity and role of Jesus is whether we focus on the teaching of Jesus as the heart and soul of his "saving" ministry, or whether we focus on the death of Jesus. We will see in chapter 7 a recent statement from the Vatican reiterating the understanding of Jesus' death as a "redeeming sacrifice ... effecting the remission of sins" and that the "whole of Christian life would be undermined" by a failure to appreciate this. In chapter 10 we will see how the August 2000 Declaration from the Vatican "On the Unicity and Salvific Universality of Jesus Christ and the Church" (*Dominus Jesus*) is reliant on Jesus being "an innocent lamb meriting life for us by his blood which he freely shed." Such statements highlight the urgent need for those of us who disagree with this focus to articulate clearly why we disagree. I believe we can disagree strongly *without* undermining the whole of Christian life. In fact, the "good news," the Gospel, can become "better news" if we rescue our understanding of Jesus and his role in human affairs from the limited and outdated worldview in which it has been traditionally presented. The fall-redemption theology that has held center stage, generally unquestioned throughout Christian history, is now suffering severely. It is tied to an outdated cosmology and anthropology, and its basic premise that humankind lost access to "heaven" lacks credibility for contemporary Western culture. Its application and relevance to other cultures is also highly questionable. The "good news" would be universally "better news" if it were linked to Jesus' preaching about the "reign of God" in our midst and the experience of the sacred in decent, everyday human actions. It is the message of Jesus, not his death, which sets us free. It is his *message* the world needs to hear. His message is "light" for our "darkness."

My experience in Australia over the past three years highlights the refusal of people in positions of authority to engage the issues and questions being raised. The common tactic of quoting authoritative sources such as Scripture, the Creed, or the *Catechism of the Catholic Church* is clearly intended to stifle discussion. This retreat into quoting sources masks a reluctance or refusal to examine the underlying assumptions and religious worldviews of the sources being quoted. Take St. Paul for example. What did he believe happened to everyone who died before Jesus? How did that belief affect what Paul believed about the saving work of Jesus? Are we still willing to hold with Paul that everyone who died before Jesus did not have access to God's "glory"? If so, why? If not, why not? It is the willingness to engage such questions that is needed rather than adopting a fixed position unwilling to budge from quoting Paul, or any other authoritative source, as the final word that ends any discussion. People operating in this fixed and closed position spare themselves the effort of engaging disturbing questions. Their theological competence is measured more by their ability to quote a section of a catechism or a passage of Scripture than by their ability to engage in respectful debate and the sharing of ideas. Such a stance also makes it easy to accuse those who ask disturbing questions of undermining Christian faith—and to make public pronouncements about their perceived errors, their ignorance of Christian tradition, and their lack of fidelity to Christian teachings.

For the past twenty years I have worked in adult faith formation. I am now more convinced than ever that some of the major causes of disruption, tension, and differences in outlook among Christians have to do with people operating from different levels or stages of faith development. There is a shameful degree of intolerance, suspicion, and condemnation existing within Christian communities simply because of a failure to appreciate various stages of adult faith development. Our basic difficulty is that most of us were never encouraged to talk about our faith, to voice our doubts and raise our questions. Christian adult faith development suffers acutely for lack of places and opportunities to tell our stories, to engage the tradition, and to wrestle with what we believe and why we believe what we freely choose to believe. We have relied so heavily on *being taught* that now in an age where everything is questioned, we find ourselves ill-equipped to handle the most basic questions being put to Christian belief. The task of providing and encouraging adults to participate in worthwhile adult faith development programs should have, I believe, equal importance with the task of providing worthwhile liturgies, instructing the young, and compassionate involvement in social concerns. It is important because

Christian faith development goes hand in hand with Christian "spirituality"—the way we hear, attend to, and articulate the story of God, God's Spirit, and Jesus and the way that story motivates the way we live and the way we gather as a Christian community.

In this time of constant change and questioning some Christians will claim to have an unshakeable faith in Absolute Truth. They may be fearful that questioning will lessen their Christian faith. This book is not for them. This book is for Christians who are touched by doubts, questioning, and even rejection of aspects of Christian faith, while still being committed to the Christian vision of life. The pity is that there are so few places where honest, open searching and questioning is respected and encouraged. Church authorities are prone to see as an attack on Christian belief what is faithfully and respectfully intended as a help to strengthen Christian faith by engagement with the issues.

The reader is invited to explore some of the fundamentals of Christian faith, to confront important issues and questions that *must be faced* if Christianity is to engage the modern world effectively. If Christianity remains tied in its images, language, and ideas to an understanding of the world and the universe that is rejected by most educated people, it will become increasingly irrelevant. It is clear this is already happening in our families and in society.

The goal of the book is the articulation—in the face of radical questioning—of a worthwhile Christian "spirituality" that is faithful to the preaching of Jesus and the Spirit at work at Pentecost and at the same time engages contemporary understanding of the universe in which we live and our lived experience. Only when we have both feet planted firmly in the ground of this spirituality will we be comfortable facing some of the challenging issues and questions confronting Christianity today.

I write as a Roman Catholic with thirty-seven years' experience in religious life and twenty-nine years of priestly ministry in education, parishes, spirituality and retreats, and adult faith development. I have resigned from priestly ministry since the publication of *Tomorrow's Catholic*. In some sections the book will allude to my Roman Catholic experience because it will help to focus on some of the key issues. I trust other Christian readers will recognize that these issues are not uniquely Roman Catholic but are relevant to all Christians wanting to participate in the conversation.

Throughout this book I use the term "Roman Catholic." Personally I prefer not to use the term. However, it is helpful for identifying a particular branch of the Christian religion since some Christians outside this particular branch identify themselves as "Catholic." The final chapter in the book will suggest that being catholic is more important than being Catholic or Roman Catholic.

Readers of *Tomorrow's Catholic* will find some repetition here. This has been necessary since the motivation for writing this book is a conviction that the issues raised in *Tomorrow's Catholic* need more open, honest, and respectful discussion among Christians. It is also necessary for readers who have not read *Tomorrow's Catholic*.

I have tried once again to write in a nonacademic style, and I acknowledge again my awareness of its limitations and its pitfalls. However, I see my task more in the vein of raising questions and stimulating conversation than in presenting an academic dissertation. This needs to be clearly understood by readers. This book is not an academic "proof" or support of a theological thesis. It is an exercise in adult faith formation and, as such, aims to engage adults in the process of wrestling with why they believe what they believe. The book will raise some thoughts and questions disturbing for some people. I am not presuming to have the answers, but I invite readers to reflect on the ideas that may be new or disturbing. It is that engagement, along with the sharing of ideas, the discussions and conversations, the grappling with what to believe and why, that is important. The Christian community can only be strengthened, not weakened, if more adult Christians articulate what it is they believe and on what grounds they believe it.

Wouldn't it be an interesting exercise if we could start afresh and attempt to formulate our understanding of Jesus in terms of contemporary knowledge of the universe and the development of life on this planet and then place this formulation and understanding beside that of the fourth-century understanding and formulation and compare the two? It would be interesting to see the results of theologians working with such freedom and to see how contemporary understanding of Jesus' identity might be similar to or might be quite different from early Christian understanding because of the dramatic change in worldview and religious imagination. Unfortunately, theologians do not enjoy such public freedom of expression. The task of contemporary, orthodox theology dealing with Jesus' identity is clearly defined as providing a contemporary interpretation of traditional doctrinal formulation. Publicly raising disturbing questions about the worldview and the reasoning processes on which traditional doctrines concerning Jesus as "true God" as well as "true man" depend is not sanctioned. Nor is any articulation of the identity of Jesus that does not conform to the traditional doctrines.

This book calls for more open, free, and honest discussion in the face of official demand for conformity. In an age of enormous confusion and questioning, an age when Christianity has to examine its basic beliefs anew and express them with clarity and in contemporary terms, we look to theologians for guidance. However, what we find again and again are theologians constrained from publicly sharing their insights and their knowledge with us. The pre–Vatican II situation is very much with us still.

In presenting the case for stepping across the boundaries and limitations of traditional doctrinal understanding of the identity of Jesus my aim is to promote discussion. Whether I am right or wrong is not the issue. The issue is whether the important questions and issues raised in these pages help people to think about their faith and about Jesus and God in an adult way. The engagement with the questions and the issues is what is important. And this is the challenge also for people who disagree strongly with me: articulate what you believe and why. Let us talk about it, discuss, explore together what we believe and why we believe it. This book invites readers to move with me into a process of adult faith formation and development.

The first step in this exercise in Christian adult faith development will examine how adult faith is generally shaped. We will examine two significant factors: (1) Christian faith begins as a *taught* faith, a faith received from significant other people, and (2) For many Christians, Christian faith is a faith reliant on the story of a "fall."

The second step will connect contemporary knowledge about the universe and the development of life on earth with the faith we acquired. We will use this "new story" of our cosmos and the development of life to reshape our images and ideas about "heaven," God's presence with us, the realities of sin and evil in our world, and the need for "salvation."

The third step will reflect on the teaching of Jesus in the light of this new story. We will see how wonderfully his teaching resonates with it. We will affirm belief in the resurrection of Jesus, but will do so with a religious imagination and an understanding of the cosmos quite different from that of the earliest Christians.

We will then engage the crucial question: Does Jesus need to be identified in a unique way with God, as "true God and true man," to "save" us? We will pose a challenge for Christians who answer "yes": articulate your answer in the framework and the language of contemporary knowledge about the universe and development of life. We will suggest that a "no" response need not undermine the Christian religion and we will examine what impact this response might have on personal faith and practice on the one hand and the institutional Christian churches on the other. We will consider some applications of this response to liturgy and ministry. Finally we will examine what a genuine catholic spirituality might be and affirm what it has to offer.

– Chapter 1 –

Adult Faith Development

W E LIVE IN AN AGE when almost everything is open to questioning. We should not be surprised that this happens in religion as it does generally in society. As adults we find ourselves challenged more and more by younger people or by our peers to justify our belief systems.

This is a significant shift for those of us who were educated in an era that did not promote or tolerate questioning. It challenges each of us to explore the basics of our Christian faith and to articulate what we believe and why.

Experts on how adults develop their faith understanding tell us we should not be surprised either by the questioning or by the challenge to justify our religious beliefs. They tell us that doubting, questioning, searching for a fresh and relevant articulation of faith, looking beyond the Christian church for further insights, wanting to take personal responsibility for what one believes, and wanting to participate in the community as someone with a voice that is heard are all basic elements of healthy adult faith development.

This needs to be more clearly understood and appreciated by Christians who have not had opportunities to engage in theological studies where processes or "stages" of adult faith development might be studied. Many Christians become disturbed by their doubts, thinking they are "losing the faith" when in fact they may well be on a personal journey to a far deeper Christian faith. What they may find on the journey, though, is that the Christian institution to which they belong is not itself moving with them or is not helping them to engage the questioning and the challenge of a personal, contemporary articulation of faith.

The following pages provide an overview of some aspects of adult faith development that have particular relevance for the way faith issues are being addressed in our Christian communities. It is not a full treatment of adult faith development, but an overview that will focus only on those aspects that have relevance for adults wanting to understand their own experience of doubts, questions, and personal articulation of faith. It will highlight some reasons for major differences of opinion, suspicion, and tension in Christian communities. It will also serve as a framework within which we will examine some critical aspects of Christian belief.

By early or late adolescence most of us had a faith identity. We were each born into families in which our parents had their religious faith, or lack of it, their opinions on a wide range of topics, their particular personalities with their gifts and limitations, their value systems, their economic situations, ethnic identities, and their plans for their children. All these factors helped to shape and nurture the beginnings of our faith journey.

We went to school and possibly began regular church attendance. We learned early in most cases that we were Christian and whether we were of the Protestant or Roman Catholic variety. As Roman Catholic Christians we would have been immersed in Roman Catholic belief and practice, or as an Anglican, Church of Christ Christian, or a member of any other Christian denomination, we would have been immersed in the beliefs and practices of those respective denominations. We learned the teachings of our church, became familiar with its rituals, and took on board devotions, prayer forms, and religious practices.

By the time we reached our teens we had already passed through several stages of faith development and acquired what some experts on faith development refer to as "conventional" faith. By this is meant a general acceptance of the faith of the "group" or religion to which we belonged. It is a faith we acquired through instruction and through the influence of significant people in our lives. Usually, it is the religious faith of our family or at least one of our parents. It is not so much a personally thought out faith as it is a faith accepted on the authority of significant people such as parents, teachers, clergy, or members of the church community. It is typically a faith untested by the trials and tribulations of life. Adult responsibilities, increased knowledge, and a growth in wisdom born of life's experiences will have much to add to this faith in future years.

The term "conventional faith" throughout this book will refer to this faith stage of acquiring knowledge about our faith, that is, what we were taught and learned from external sources of authority entrusted with teaching us "the faith" of our particular religion. It is a stage of faith development in which people "learn" the basics of belief. Religious education of children generally strives to provide a solid grounding in this conventional stage of faith. With its emphasis on initiation and learning it is obviously both a good and necessary stage. To neglect it would be to build faith on sand since there would be no link with the teaching, the beliefs, the authority, the community, and the "reason for being" of the religious group.

Ideally, however, this stage is but a stepping stone toward a more mature faith in which people bring their own thoughtful reflection, increased knowledge, personal experience of life, and their powers of critical reasoning to reexamine the faith they have acquired. People then believe not only on the basis of having been taught to believe something, but because they have thought about it and can articulate their reasons for believing and wanting to live in that faith. Failure to move on to this more mature level of faith can result in adult faith with childish, dependent characteristics. It can leave people dependent on others for what they believe. It can also create a gap in people's lives between the faith they have learned and their lived experience because they will not allow new knowledge or their lived experience to question the faith package they have been taught. This failure to move on is evident among Christians today. We see it expressed in the cry, "But this is what I was taught to believe!" when adult Christians find it difficult to accept insights, knowledge, or understandings different from the conventional faith they acquired in their earlier religious education.

We need to recognize that any of us can still be at the conventional faith level on some aspects of faith even though we may have moved beyond this level on many significant aspects of faith. Don't we occasionally find ourselves thinking or saying, "I've never thought about that!" when someone presents a new way of thinking about some item of faith we have held, unchallenged, since childhood days?

If adult faith is arrested at this conventional stage or at an even earlier stage of development, some of the following characteristics may operate strongly in the adult's approach to faith issues:

• Literal belief in the myths and the stories learned in childhood. The best example is the Adam and Eve story. The "story" becomes fact. "This is what I was taught to believe!" Faith and a whole theological system become based on this supposed "fact." Anyone challenging such literal belief is seen to be challenging the authority of people who taught in the name of the church.

- Literal interpretation of symbols. A good example is Roman Catholics who, contrary to Roman Catholic sacramental theology, believe the consecrated bread at Eucharist is actually a physical, bodily presence of Jesus.

- Literal understanding of scriptural events that are clearly dealing with mystery, for example, the belief that Jesus' physical body actually rose up into the sky after the resurrection and went to "heaven."

- Uncritical loyalty to external authority; not trusting in one's own right or capacity to make decisions impinging on belief or morality. People continue to depend on authority figures to guide them and to provide answers to life's questions.

- Unquestioning acceptance of dogma and doctrine. This manifests itself in dogmatism that is unable to provide reasons for belief.

- Fear of changing from what was taught. Reliance on external authority results in weak personal faith identity. The individual does not have sufficient confidence to take personal responsibility for reconstructing his or her theological beliefs.

- Literal belief in hell and heaven as places, purgatory, and a judgment at death. People hold on to their childhood images of what meeting God at the time of death might be like.

- Faith in devotions that work much like magic. Include here any religious devotions that presume God's love, presence, or intervention can be attained by using a particular formula or ritual.

- Mistrust of scholarship that disturbs one's religious worldview.

- Naïve historical understanding. Most Christians, even the most liberal, are extraordinarily historically naïve or ignorant about how thinking and practices developed within their religious denomination. Many adult Roman Catholics, for example, presume Jesus instituted individual confession to a priest, whereas it was unknown in early Christian centuries.

- Claims of exclusivity: we are the only true religion. People stay locked into their childhood identification with one particular religious group and are not able to appreciate that all of humankind shares the one Transcendent Spirit. Consequently, they resist thinking through the implications of the universality of God's presence.

- Expectations of conformity and uniformity.

- Strict adherence to laws and rules. Some people cannot see beyond laws and regulations. They complain to authority figures when someone contravenes or steps around a law. This is especially true for liturgical regulations.

- The persistence of childhood images of God as the framework for prayer, worship, and thinking. For example, God is male, external, and looks "down" on us. God will punish bad people. God will love us more if we do more good things. God reacts. God can do anything. God locked us out of heaven. God sent His Son down from heaven because Adam and Eve sinned. Childhood belief becomes adult conviction.

- Strict sexual morality. Childhood taboos about sex carry over into adulthood.

- Glorifying the past; believing that a return to the past would solve today's problems. If only we had good religious instruction in our schools! If only religious education teachers today were like the teachers we had!

- The equating of "church" with the teaching authority rather than with the body of believers. Children usually do not identify themselves as "the church," and this lack of identification carries into adulthood. There is stress on, "The church says..." "The church teaches..." rather than developing awareness of and responsibility for God's Spirit at work in their lives and being "church."

- A lack of understanding of how the four Gospels were formed. This leaves people with the belief that Jesus actually spoke every word attributed to him.

- Ignorant defense of the faith. In extreme cases some people who are locked into this stage of faith development agitate against scholars and educators who they believe are undermining their traditional belief system. It is not unusual to find, for example, people with no academic qualifications in theology or Scripture studies ready to argue publicly with scholars in these fields simply because something different to what they learned years ago is being expressed.

A sad feature of contemporary institutionalized religion is that adults are kept at the conventional stage of faith rather than being led to or encouraged to a deeper faith. This reflects a widespread institutional attitude that "true" faith is found in the uncritical acceptance of what has been taught rather than in the search to make faith meaningful in a world full of challenges.

In the absence of official support and encouragement, how do we move beyond conventional faith? Basically, we move on when we allow events in life to raise questions about what we believe and why. A personal experience, a conversation with a friend, a sudden insight or further education can cause us, if we allow it, to examine particular aspects of what we believe. For example, a middle-aged Roman Catholic couple might have always believed that divorced persons who did not have their marriage annulled should not be admitted to Communion if they married again. However, they begin to think differently when their married daughter decides to divorce her violent husband. When she, without grounds for annulment, marries again, her parents must confront their long-held beliefs about such situations. Their daughter's circumstances of being a victim of abuse leads them to conclude that church law should not punish her by refusing her the right to receive Communion.

One of the biggest shifts in the Roman Catholic community occurred with the papal ban on contraception in marriage. Conscience and the formation of conscience became a most important issue. Adults found themselves being challenged by the situation to think through how they would respond and why.

This movement beyond conventional faith can begin at any point from our late teens onward. The process invites us to consider seriously our reasons for believing what we believe and why we choose to act the way we do. We *think through* our faith and our actions in the light of our lived experience and personally take responsibility for accepting or rejecting particular aspects of belief. We seek to make faith *ours*.

An essential feature of being an adult lies in accepting responsibility for one's beliefs and actions. An "adult" Christian ought to be a Christian not simply because of being born into a Christian family. At some stage in our adult life we have to take personal responsibility for being a Christian. Essential to this responsibility is being able to articulate what we believe and why we are prepared to keep on believing it. Faith is deepened when we have personally thought it through, seen its truth, wisdom, or value, and have affirmed its importance for the way we live.

The ideal situation would be for all adult members of a

particular religious group to move into and through this stage of personal critical examination of what they believe, and to emerge from it still believing everything they had been taught at the "conventional" educative stage.

But it is obvious to all of us that this is not what happens. Our own experience gives witness to this. Many of us no longer believe everything we were taught to believe.

Many of us, with due respect to the teaching authority of our respective churches, disagree on some aspects of belief, law, or moral teaching from that authority. We are aware that wide differences of belief exist even within particular branches of Christianity. Some Anglicans believe in angels; some don't. Some Christians readily accept divorce and remarriage; others do not. Some Christians believe Jesus had brothers and sisters; others believe he was an only child. Some Roman Catholics believe in a place called purgatory; others no longer believe in such a place. We could go on and find many other examples. What is significant is that questioning particular items of conventional belief does not necessarily sever commitment to our religion. Indeed, many of us know through personal experience that taking responsibility for what we are prepared to believe or discard has strengthened our commitment.

One risk in this movement to articulate what we are prepared to believe is that of associating only with others who think as we do. We can lock ourselves into "movements," "causes," "isms," or groups which have led us into insights and deeper understanding but which now become the answer to all of faith's questions. Association with a reform or renewal group, for example, may bring insights, meaning, understanding, and even development of personal identity and responsibility. However, the risk is that we become too one-sided or one-dimensional in our approach to faith because we look only through the lens of the group's concerns or think only in the thought patterns of the group.

A second risk is that of being caught up into what "I think."
What "I think" can be pretty shallow at times, especially if we
have not been exposed to the thinking and values that shaped
traditional faith. For example, how many Roman Catholics
have read or have a good understanding of the papal encycli-
cal banning contraception in marriage? How many simply
reacted with, "The pope is not going to tell me what I can
or cannot do in my bedroom!"? How many, on the other
hand, were motivated by the situation to articulate the values
important to them, their marriages, and their own particular
circumstances and to bring this articulation into respectful
dialogue with a clear church teaching, and then choose to
dissent from the teaching or assent to it?

Entrance into this stage of personal, critical (in a good
sense) evaluation and articulation of faith carries the risk of
the baby being thrown out with the bath water. A common
example of this occurs in the context of Christians discovering that the Adam and Eve story is not to be taken literally.
Some people overreact, discarding their Christian faith alto-
gether on the grounds their faith was built on what they now
think was "a lie" taught to them. Others wonder if they can
ever trust the truth of Scripture again.

This highlights the need for access to scholarship as people
move from conventional faith into stages of questioning and
reflection. For example, the movement from literal understanding of some scriptural stories needs to be accompanied
with an adult appreciation of myth, the formation of Scripture, the way revelation occurs, and access to Christian
biblical scholarship. Often, though, none of this is on hand,
and people are left with a faith that has fallen apart. In their
disillusionment, some may ask why they should believe any-
more when what they thought was unchangeable truth and
the bedrock of their faith has changed.

One of the essential characteristics of this maturing stage

of faith is the willingness and the ability to allow our experience of life and our faith questions to dialogue with the teaching tradition and scholarship of the church community. Without the balance this dialogue promotes, we risk falling into either, "No one is going to tell me what to believe and do"—overemphasizing our personal experience and thinking; or "I expect the church to tell me what I am to believe and do"—overemphasizing church authority.

The urgency for this type of dialogue presents a challenge for institutional Christianity in its approach to adult faith formation. In the past it managed to relate with both children and adults at a conventional faith stage, relying on instruction and the power of its authority to ensure allegiance. The independent thinking stage of faith with its critical reasoning and examination of data belonged more to theologians and academics. But Western society in general has now moved into this questioning stage. If Christianity wants to remain relevant, it needs to meet people where they are. The institution's general attitude and one-sided practice of instruction and command, which worked well in the past, will not work for people at this stage of their faith development.

Good teachers are important, but more important for this task are adult faith educators, men and women conversant with the teaching of the church and skilled in processes that enable adults to share and learn.

Every local church community will need to address this challenge by providing places and opportunities for people to share their faith experiences, their questions and doubts, and to bring these into dialogue with the teaching of the church. This need is as important as providing parish liturgies, for without faith being nourished and deepened, liturgy becomes lifeless. We Christians are fooling ourselves and doing our religion a grave disservice if we imagine we can keep Christian faith strong and dynamic among adults by concentrating on a conventional faith model of church. We need far more than traditional religious 'instruction and an unchanging liturgy to keep the faith alive today.

However, it is very difficult to convince Christians who are firmly at the conventional stage of faith and who are in the majority in many places of Christian worship to see the need for change. Their faith is strong. In fact, they believe if more people had faith like theirs, the church would be healthy and strong! Their attitude is that all this questioning cannot be good for the church, that it would be better to let the "disturbed" people drift away and leave them in peace. They cannot understand how people can call themselves Christians and raise questions about doctrine and accepted Christian practice.

In many local church communities tension between adults who remain at the conventional stage of faith development and those who are moving beyond that stage is evident. The tension is increased when the faith level of the ordained leader of the community differs from that of significant and influential people in the community. A pastoral leader steeped in conventional faith is likely to be frustrated and concerned if most members of the pastoral board or team have moved beyond that stage of faith. The board members are also likely to feel frustrated and concerned because the pastoral leader does not share their dream of what the parish might be. Conversely, misunderstanding and discord are almost inevitable if a pastoral leader wants to lead the community beyond the conventional stage of faith and finds his or her vision of how the community could operate is not shared by people at that conventional faith stage.

There are further levels of faith development beyond the two described here. Again, movement usually begins when a significant disruption occurs, causing people to look at life, themselves, and other people differently. Something happens to the way they think, see, and judge. Something happens causing them to see reality from a new perspective.

Two key elements in the further development of faith are:

- A recognition that truth, wisdom, insight, and understanding can and must be approached from different perspectives. There are polarities or opposites to be balanced and respected, and people come to appreciate how one-sided they may have been in the past in their approach to "truth." Logic, reason, and knowledge need to be balanced with compassion, sensitivity, and tolerance. The past balanced with the present. Law with values. Jesus as someone radically different from us with Jesus as someone radically like us. There is much wisdom to be discovered if people break out of a one-sided approach to reality. This is especially true for anyone who, at the previous stage of faith development, got locked into "movements," "causes," and "isms" in which they thought they had found or would find all the answers to life's problems and questions.

- A movement to identify with people unlike themselves. This is a movement toward becoming more universalistic in thinking and in action. It breaks across ethnic, cultural, and religious boundaries in an appreciation that all human beings are bonded. This is a big step to take because it challenges previously strongly ingrained ethnic, cultural, and religious notions of identity and exclusive relationship with God. Thinking and acting is now conducted in the context of all people being God's people.

This need for balance and for being able to think beyond the boundaries in which we have been accustomed to think has relevance for academics and church leaders. They can become experts in their own particular fields of study, surrounding themselves with like-minded thinkers, living and thinking in their own theological and religious understandings, and not exposing themselves to views, knowledge, and insights from other fields of learning or from other cultures. Advanced learning and expertise in a particular academic field—even if it be theology—should not be confused with adult faith development.

Roman Catholicism as an "ism" has generally resisted movement to these further stages of faith development, preferring to proclaim itself as the bearer of absolute truth. Individual Roman Catholics, on the other hand, enter into this further stage of faith development embracing serious dialogue with and a willingness to learn from other religious traditions. They find they can do this and enrich their faith. Some find the Roman Catholic expression of religious faith too narrow, too insular and limiting, too concerned about the "Roman Catholic" world, too locked into the past, its rituals irrelevant to the concerns of the contemporary world, and so they cut themselves off from the Roman Catholic institutional expressions of religion.

Roman Catholics who move to this level of faith do not necessarily stop being Roman Catholic, but want to explore more deeply the reality of God at work in all people, in all cultures and places, in all religions, at all times. As they explore they find that their sense of alienation and their search are shared by Christians of other traditions and people of other religious faiths who are experiencing a similar movement in their faith development.

A challenge here is to articulate a shared human experience of the Transcendent Reality that Christians name "God." As this challenge is engaged people find themselves moving from the framework of stories particular to one culture or religious tradition, such as the story of Adam and Eve's fall from grace. They find themselves articulating their religious faith within the framework of a much wider and more universally accepted understanding of the universe in which we live, of how life developed on this planet, and the belief that God's creative Spirit has always been present in creation. It is in this broader perspective that many Christians seek to discuss their questions about God, evil, suffering, sin, the wonder of life, the purpose of human existence, death, and the identity and role of Jesus of Nazareth.

Discussion Points

1. Who were your most significant educators into conventional faith? What aspects of teaching remain strong in your memory?

2. What was the first major shift in your adult Christian thought or conduct? Who or what prompted the shift?

3. What has been your most recent shift? Who or what prompted it?

4. Which, if any, of the factors listed on pages 20–23 have had particular significance or application in your own faith journey?

5. In what ways are the tensions between various levels of faith development evident in your local or broader church community?

– Chapter 2 –

A New Story for
Theology and Spirituality

W HEN WE REFLECT on the way we were nurtured into
our Christian faith, most of us would recognize a
common pattern. In our childhood we learned the Genesis
stories about creation and a "fall." We learned to interpret
the Old Testament as the "story of salvation," God's way of
preparing humankind for the coming of the Savior. We were
immersed in the story of Jesus as God's "Son," who restored
what Adam and Eve had lost. We came to understand that
the church was founded by Jesus to preach the good news
and to ensure that "salvation"—generally understood as access to heaven—was available to all of humankind. We also
became increasingly aware that there were different Christian
churches and that ours was the "right" one.

Immersed in this faith perspective we entered adulthood,
conscious of our commitment to a particular Christian church,
and we looked at the world around us through the lens of this
church. Most of us carried into adulthood convictions that
our branch of the Christian church was right on key aspects
of religious belief and practice and that other branches and
other religions were at best misguided, if not wrong. In our
eyes, these convictions gave our church a special standing when
compared with other churches and other religions. We were

convinced our Christian church possessed religious truth, free from error.

The basic elements of this faith approach to the world may be summarized as follows:

The Genesis stories of creation and a fall

God prepares the way for a Savior

Jesus restores what was lost

The church is the medium for "salvation"

Our particular church is the only one free from error

We engage the world around us
shaped in our Christian religious convictions

The key factor for our consideration here is that we came to engage the world around us as members of a particular Christian church. Our formation in the beliefs and practices of this church influenced our attitude to the world and to people of different faiths. What many of us then tried to do, even if unwittingly, was to fit the rest of the world and all other people into our religious categories of thinking. We tried to fit everything into our Christian story.

This process has also been followed by Christian theologians throughout the centuries. Christian thinkers in the early centuries of Christianity wrestled with questions regarding the role of Jesus and his identity. They did so in the context of a "fall" and in the understanding that Jesus was God's gracious response to restore what human beings had lost through the "fall" of Adam and Eve. The great church councils of the fourth and fifth centuries formulated doctrines that gave "orthodox" answers to the questions that arose from that context and understanding. This doctrinal teaching was formulated in precise and technical language and became the framework and the guarantor of "correct" Christian thinking and teaching. Generally, Christian theologizing has been done, and is being done, within the framework of these doctrinal definitions. Most branches of the Christian church have developed institutionalized ways to ensure that only "correct" teaching, within the framework of those doctrinal definitions, is taught. The magisterium of the Roman Catholic Church is perhaps the best example of a governing body safeguarding what it determines to be orthodox teaching and ensuring that Roman Catholic theologians stay within acceptable, traditional boundaries. The magisterium, armed with its "correct" doctrine—to the point of believing it to be absolute, unquestionable truth—requires that Roman Catholic speculative theology remain within the traditional theological framework while examining contemporary issues and questions. God's activity in the non-Christian world and all of the universe has been interpreted and generally is still being interpreted through a Christian lens, and this lens is taken to be the only acceptable way of interpreting God's activity.

But this lens has an extremely narrow focus. The focus has been on a particular, culturally conditioned story of creation and a fall from an original state of "paradise." We shall see in the pages to come that the magisterium still demands that contemporary understanding of God's activity in our known universe, our present-day knowledge of the development of life on this planet, and serious acceptance of God's activity in all places, at all times, in all peoples has to be understood and taught within a quite limited and outdated understanding of creation, a fall, and God's plan for salvation. This demand is impossible to achieve. It is like trying to squeeze a beach ball into a golf ball. It is like trying to put new wine into old wineskins and discovering there are leaks everywhere.

What if Christian theology shifted its starting point? What if, instead of beginning with its traditional understanding of creation and a fall from paradise, it began with a much bigger, wider, more global and universal story of creation? What if it began with what writers call "The New Story" or "The New Cosmology"? By this they are referring to the generally accepted scientific understanding of the formation and size of our universe, the formation of this planet, and the development of life on it. The term "New Story" will be used throughout this book with this meaning. There is no intent here to present contemporary scientific understanding as unchangeable fact, for we will surely learn more and more in the years ahead. Nor is scientific data presented here for its own sake. Rather the data will be used as a basis for this "New Story," a story to tell us afresh who we are in this universe in which we live. The focus will be on how contemporary knowledge of the formation of our universe, its size, the formation of planets, the beginnings of life, and the development of life on this planet can lead us into mystery, wonder, wisdom, insight, care, concern—and all the elements that help to give meaning and purpose to our lives. The New Story, unlike all other prior stories in human history about the formation of the universe, is now available to people in all places, in all cultures. In this context we can reflect on our images of God, where we would expect to encounter God's presence, what humankind's basic relationship with God might be, and where Jesus fits into this story.

We bring to this New Story the belief that God's creative Spirit has always been present and active at all times and in all places in this vast universe; present and active during the billions of years of life on this planet before human life emerged; present and active in all places, in all cultures, in all people, and throughout all of human history. Is this too much for us to believe as Christians?

Immersing ourselves in the New Story and our belief in
the active presence of God's Spirit will have enormous consequences for the way we shape contemporary Christian faith.
A significant new starting point and development will be:

Contemporary scientific understanding of the universe
and the development of life on earth

God present and active in all places at all times

*The Spirit of God working in
and becoming visible through:*

The material universe

The development of life

The development of human culture

The human attributes of love, generosity,
caring, compassion, forgiveness

If we choose to think about Jesus within the context of
this framework and use it to reflect on his identity and role
in human "salvation," we need to understand that we may
be led to conclusions not shared by people who think and
operate out of the framework outlined on page 33.

The New Story challenges those who believe in the separation of heaven and earth, who think in terms of human
beings emerging into a state of paradise, who take literally
the idea that a body can rise up into the sky and go somewhere, who think in terms of "heaven" as a place above us
where God resides, who believe God's activity is focused on
one religious group.

The New Story and belief in the Spirit's active presence
also challenge "official" Christian teaching as contained in

the precise and technical language of the great early councils of the church.

So why pursue this New Story, why raise difficult questions, why suggest radical changes to the way we articulate our Christian faith?

The answer is found in the belief that the New Story can help to make the experience of God revealed in Jesus more relevant to our world today. People at a particular time of history witnessed in Jesus an experience of God's presence in their midst, in a human person. They believed that in this man, Jesus, they had seen, heard, touched, and been touched by God in a way that made Jesus central to their understanding of who God is and what God is like. God came to perfect human expression in this man. Jesus incarnated "put flesh on" the Unseen and Unknowable God. We want to engage this story, and we want to make this story relevant to our times. If we refuse to engage the challenge of doing this in the images, concepts, language, and data universally accepted in our time, then we are not protecting the wonderful good news of Jesus; we are consigning it to irrelevancy. The experience of God we have come to know in Jesus demands that we engage the challenge. We have to do so as diligently and as courageously—and probably with as much dispute and argumentation!—as the Christian thinkers in the early centuries of the church engaged a similar challenge.

However, many devout Christians are resisting this challenge. They seem to think the Christian story will be better protected and enlivened if they cling to past frameworks of interpreting the saving work of Jesus. Hold on to what is familiar. Hold on to what we were taught. Be suspicious of the questioning for it will undermine the foundations of the church. Yet their response, which seems so reasonable and so loyal to the church, will ensure that Christian faith does not engage either the lived experience or the contemporary worldview of many adult Christians.

There is no doubt that the New Story will attract strong criticism, suspicion, and alienation from powerful authority figures as well as from some members of our churches with whom we share pews on Sundays. But it is worth the risk.

It is worth the risk because the truth will set us free. Christianity has nothing to lose and everything to gain by proclaiming the message of Jesus and the experience of Pentecost in the images, language, knowledge, concerns, and longings of this present century. The task of reaching into the Jesus story and bringing its universal applications to the lived experience of people today cannot and should not be avoided.

It is worth doing because in the doing we will inevitably address one of the biggest shifts in the history of Christianity. This is the widespread phenomenon of many adult Christians wrestling with and discarding the "package" in which their conventional faith was grounded. Many know and can articulate aspects of that package to which they are no longer willing to give credence. Two concerns frequently emerge for people caught in the shift.

The first concern is: what do we believe now? Many of their questions touch the very foundations of Christian faith. They are questions about the nature and presence of God, questions about "redemption," questions about God's forgiveness being dependent on Jesus dying on a cross, questions about divinity and humanity, questions about the role of church authority, questions about the status of and respect to be given to individual conscience. People are looking for an alternative articulation of Christian faith that is not reliant on a religious worldview they have discarded.

The second concern is: can we still call ourselves Roman Catholic or Christian if our articulation of faith is radically different from the way our church has taught us to think?

These concerns connect with current misunderstandings concerning "spirituality" and "tradition." Christian spirituality is the way people bring their understanding of God, God's Spirit, and Jesus to their lived experience. If Christian spirituality is to be strong and dynamic, it must be able to bring the story of Jesus and his teaching about God to people in the context of today's world and contemporary knowledge about the world and the universe. Christians must be attentive both to the story of Jesus and to today's world. Tradition is the record of how people did this in the past, and its wisdom is handed down from age to age to help the present age be attentive.

Our current difficulty is to mistake a particular theological framework as *the* tradition, as if the framework is immutable and beyond questioning. The framework for traditional Christian thinking has been the fall-redemption. Many people today reject that framework and any theological conclusions reliant on it, even though these doctrinal conclusions are presented as the "tradition." Yes, they are the "tradition" in the sense of being handed down from generation to generation, but it is significant that the task of tradition—and this age will be part of the church's "tradition" in another thousand years—is to hand on how a particular age kept alive and preached the story of Jesus to the world it encountered.

What many people today are rejecting in their spirituality is an outmoded framework as they try to be attentive and faithful to the story of Jesus and their contemporary situation. What they experience is that the church community, in its teaching and liturgy, remains firmly anchored in the old framework and is not supportive of their spirituality that develops along with their faith.

The "New Story," the "New Cosmology" provides a new framework in which people can reflect on God, God's Spirit, and the story of Jesus and bring that reflection to their lived experience and knowledge about life and the universe. This

New Story is well known throughout the world. Television documentaries focus on various aspects of this story: the planets, the formation of stars, how the universe was formed, the size of the universe, black holes, the development of life on earth, the search for life on other planets, to name just a few. Elementary school libraries have a wide range of resources that nurture today's children into a wonderful story about the universe that was unknown to us when we were children. Many writers use the data and insights that emerge from this story to comment on ecological concerns, especially to address the harm human beings have done to this planet. The New Story has the capacity to fire imagination and to instill a sense of wonder and awe in anyone open to the marvels of our universe.

In the light of the accessibility and wide acceptance of this story of the universe it is striking how few theologians have put into writing the implications for Christian theology. That they know the implications, if they know the "story," is beyond doubt. But there appears to be an air of intellectual dishonesty created by authoritarian insistence on fidelity to "Tradition." Christian churches that profess to seek and to be open to "all truth" have a way of saying, "We have all truth, thank you, and nothing you can say can lead us beyond the boundaries and technical language in which we have enshrined our truth. And if anything you say, teach, or write seems to cross the boundaries we have set, we will ensure that you lose your right to speak, teach, and write in the name of the church." The Roman Catholic Church, for example, insists that teachers of theology make a profession of faith which concludes, "I adhere with religious submission of will and intellect to the teachings which either the Roman Pontiff or the College of Bishops enunciate when they exercise their authentic magisterium, even if they do not intend to proclaim these teachings by a definitive act."

So it is not an easy task we want to engage, nor is it one for which institutional leadership will give support and encouragement. It will perhaps open us to profoundly disturbing questions, questions without immediate or ready-made answers. But we move into the task for the sake of making the experience of God revealed in Jesus "good news" for our lives and our world. We know we are not the first generation of Christians struggling to find adequate, yet inevitably inadequate, words and images to proclaim the "good news" of Jesus' life and teaching. Consider the influence of Paul in the way Christianity interacted with non-Jewish believers, the influence of the Greek "fathers of the church" making the Christian message relevant to the prevailing philosophies and worldviews of the times, the way Augustine made use of Neo-Platonism, and St. Thomas Aquinas's reliance on the Greek philosopher Aristotle as a medium for conducting the Christian message of "good news" for the world.

The reality is Christianity cannot insist that the final word on Jesus has been spoken and that language and ideas of one century are to hold for all time. The Christian church has a responsibility, surely, to use the images, language, and story available to it at any time in history. The New Story proposed here will in time be significantly modified. Most of the matter that makes up our universe is still undiscovered and unknown; we do not know whether ours is the only universe; we do not know where life originated, and we know very little about life outside of our galaxy. We do not yet understand how the human brain works in making decisions or holding images. Future discoveries will surely bring further insights into God's creative presence and will impinge on the way we relate the story of Jesus of Nazareth.

Nor is it only the New Story that the Christian church must engage in helping people encounter the reality of God revealed in Jesus. It has to consider, for example, what postmodernist or feminist thinking brings to the encounter. It has to consider also what difference social and economic situations make to the way people encounter the story of Jesus and how they respond to it.

People living two thousand years in the future will face the same challenge we face today in making the story of Jesus relevant to their time. Their "world" and their scientific data will be as different from ours as ours is from the days of the Roman empire.

It seems abundantly clear that if Christians keep thinking and acting as if the language, images, and worldview of fourth-century Christianity is the only acceptable way to tell the story of Jesus, Christianity will have little to contribute to the continuing story of God's Spirit at work in our universe, on our planet, and in every human life.

Discussion Points

1. Is there any aspect of contemporary scientific knowledge about the universe, earth, and the development of life that raises questions for you about the framework in which Christian faith has been handed down through the centuries?

2. What are your questions concerning where God is and how human beings relate with God?

– Chapter 3 –

Re-forming Our Imagination

TRADITIONAL CHRISTIAN FAITH has provided us with ways of understanding a wide range of religious topics, such as God's relationship with creation, heaven, original sin, revelation, salvation, Jesus human and divine, and the place of the Christian religion among other religions. We now want to engage the challenge of moving from the framework in which that faith was grounded to the "New Story" as a contemporary way to ground our Christian faith. We do so in the interest of making faith reasonable and able to stand up to the searching questions raised by contemporary knowledge about our universe and the development of life on our planet. Mature, adult, personally appropriated faith will ignore neither the knowledge nor the questions.

Our modern-day understanding of the universe provides us with the opportunity to appreciate that God is way beyond our imagining—far more so than for the Hebrew people of Old Testament times or for the Christians who shaped doctrinal formulations in the early centuries of Christianity. Their understanding of the universe was very, very limited, and in a real sense their God was smaller than ours. Our concepts of time and space deal with billions of years and billions of galaxies in an ever-expanding universe. They thought in terms of an enclosed cosmos. And Christian thinkers naturally interpreted the life and death of Jesus within that enclosed cosmos framework.

The following factors are important in the way the story of Jesus has traditionally been told. First, the understanding of the physical universe. Many people at the time of Jesus thought in terms of a three-tiered universe. Heaven, the dwelling place of God, or gods, was a place above, on the top tier. Earth was in the middle and was considered to be the center of the universe. Hebrew thought imagined a flat earth held in place by pillars descending into the seas. Underneath the earth was literally the "underworld," the place of darkness, and many people considered it was the place where the powers of evil dwelled.

Second, the Hebrew story of creation. It was not intended to be a scientific explanation. The creation story in Genesis arose from people of a particular religious culture wrestling with very important questions about life and about God. They believed that God is Good and Almighty, and that God made everything "good" at the time of creation. God did not make anything "bad." However, their experience of upheaval, disasters, calamities, and tragedies of all kinds led them to believe something had gone wrong. Whatever had gone wrong could not be God's doing or God's intent because God is perfectly Good and Almighty. Furthermore, God created the first human beings "good." How, then, were they to account for the harmful behavior of human beings—the killing, the stealing, the raping, the lack of awareness of God? Clearly the reason had to lie in human beings turning aside from the "good" state in which God had created them.

So the Adam and Eve story was told. It was a story trying to make sense of reality and to do justice to a fundamental belief in the utter goodness of the Creator.

However, when this story became accepted as factual, as

actually describing what happened at the beginning of human history, it created images of a punishing God and of human beings living under that punishment. Further, when this story was superimposed on a three-tiered understanding of the universe, it cemented images and ideas of human beings cutting themselves off from access to God. Heaven was closed to them. And human beings were considered powerless to bridge the gap they had created through their own fault.

Third, the religious and philosophical dualism prevalent in Greek culture. Dualism contrasts two realities set against one another such as: mind-matter or soul-body. Part of the dualistic thinking of the time conceived of a separation between heaven and earth. Some religious movements influenced by dualism considered earth to be a place of exile and the body to be a prison for the soul. Some people believed there were two powers competing for control of the universe, one good and the other evil. There was also a belief that what was real existed in another realm and what is experienced on earth is only a shadowy representation of what existed in true form elsewhere. There was great interest in that other realm and in how some people could gain access to it by special knowledge. The non-Christian world, in trying to make sense of human existence, was asking questions for which Christianity thought it had answers.

Christians believed the story of Jesus heralded the good news that the separation between heaven and earth had been bridged. In Jesus, humanity had someone who had access to God's dwelling place. Jesus opened the gates of heaven! Jesus restored humankind to friendship with God! Jesus won forgiveness for humanity's sins!

There was a clear understanding that Jesus made possible something that would not have been possible without him. He was the perfect answer to humankind's questions about the meaning of life, human destiny, life after death, and access

to heaven. Jesus brought "salvation" to a world that desperately needed to hear a message of hope and the wonderful
possibility of eternal life with God after death.

We look at that understanding today with great respect.
We recognize that the story of Jesus had to be told within the
context of the prevailing worldview.

Today, however, we have ways of understanding God that
were not accessible to people living centuries before us, and
we are being challenged to allow these ways to enlighten
us and to move us forward in our understanding of God's
presence and activity in creation.

Let us look first at the way we are exposed today to a
new understanding of the universe, an understanding far, far
removed from the three-tiered universe of the past. Let us
consider how concepts such as "everywhere" and "all times"
are literally light years away from past understandings.

We have a better appreciation today of the vastness of our
universe, a universe with billions and billions of galaxies.
Each galaxy has billions and billions of stars. One way to
appreciate the vastness is to think about the star we call our
"sun" and the system of planets, including earth, dependent
on it. Think about the light from this one star and its extent.
Think about the fact that human beings are never (as far as
we know from present knowledge) likely to travel outside of
the influence of this one star. We are not even likely to travel
far inside our solar system. And here we are talking about
one star in the Milky Way galaxy that contains hundreds of
billions of stars. What about all those other stars? April 1999
brought news of the discovery within our galaxy of the first
solar system other than our own—three planets orbiting a star
called Upsilon Andromedae. This star is roughly three billion
years old, two-thirds the age of our sun. It would take us
thousands of years to travel to this star. Astronomers believe
there may be an abundance of planetary systems associated

with the two hundred billion stars in our galaxy. Then we have several hundred billion other galaxies to consider, each with hundreds of billions of stars.

For Christians, this type of scientific data has significant theological implications. In the face of such awe-inspiring data, what happens to our image of God or to the way we might think about God? What does it mean to say, "God is everywhere." What does it mean to say that God's creative Spirit has been active *in all places at all times* in this universe?

We can not ignore the implications for the way we think about God when we engage in this reflection and contemplation. God is not situated in one place. God is not more present in one place than somewhere else. God is not present in some places and absent elsewhere in this universe. Nothing can exist without God's presence sustaining it in existence. God is not here *or* there. While someone might choose to live in an understanding that God is absent, in fact God cannot be absent. That has always been part of Christianity's understanding of God. Everything that has existence exists *in* God.

So let God be *everywhere*. Let us give up any conventional faith images that present God as a localized "person" dwelling somewhere above, looking down on us.

What impact might this have on a conventional faith understanding of heaven and life after death?

Many Christians have been nurtured with images of heaven as a place above us, "somewhere else," and that at death the "soul" begins a journey to that place and God's judgment will decide whether entry will be granted. This popular image links this "somewhere else" understanding of heaven with "God's dwelling place." But if heaven is wherever God is, our reflection on the vastness of our universe has something new to tell us about where heaven might be. God and heaven are not somewhere else. Our death will not be a journey somewhere. Rather it will be a transformation into a completely different way of living *in* God, God always present in creation.

This has significant implications for those Christians who take literally the story of the "fall" of Adam and Eve from paradise, God "locking the gates of heaven" and all the redemption theology dependent on this understanding. If we stop thinking of heaven as a *place* existing somewhere else, our watertight theological understanding of Jesus who "opens the gates of heaven" for us begins to leak. What we have instead is the belief that God is everywhere, and nothing, absolutely nothing, can change that. We Christians believe we live *in* God; we believe we will die *in* God. Images of descending and ascending lose relevance and any sense in this perspective. We live *in* God now, and in death we will be *living on in God*. The manner of this "living on" is completely unknown to us, but at least we can rule out the images of souls floating up into the sky and being greeted by Someone who decides whether they are going to be admitted into a place called "heaven." We can also rule out images and ideas about the "gates of heaven being locked."

How were these conventional images formed in us? Which images have been the most powerful for us? Do we still imagine that death is a journey to a place somewhere else? Do we still imagine or believe that the "gates of heaven" were locked? If so, what are we imagining "heaven" to be, and how is it possible for access to be "locked"? When we engage such questions we are moving beyond a level of faith that unquestioningly accepted the framework in which our faith was nurtured. The questions may be disturbing, but at the same time they have the capacity to make faith more real for us. They help us to see that some movement and growth in our understanding are called for if faith is to be adult and reasonable.

Many of us have been strongly influenced by religious language about "the next world" and by the notion that our lives here on earth are an "exile" from the place where God dwells. We also find that ideas and images formed in childhood are deeply entrenched. However, we cannot afford the luxury of staying with these notions because they will not sustain faith for future generations of Christians. We adult Christians should challenge images of human beings living in "exile" from God if we want to enliven our own faith and the faith of future generations of Christian believers.

Traditional Christianity teaches that "the gates of heaven were locked," that humankind lost access to eternal life with God, and that human beings were in exile from God because of the sin of the first human beings. Let us consider how this faith understanding developed before we consider how contemporary knowledge of the development of life on earth might suggest a shift in understanding.

Paul, preaching and writing about twenty years after the death of Jesus, had a profound influence on Christian understanding and interpretation of Jesus' salvific work. Paul believed that because of Adam's sin, death came into the world. This "death" is not just a physical death. It is a death that blocked access to God. Human sin set up this state of "death" or separation from God. Paul taught that Jesus is our "savior" because he broke the hold of "death" on us and restored human access to eternal life with God. In Paul's understanding, Jesus "was handed over to death for our trespasses and was raised for our justification" (Rom. 4:25)

While we were still weak, at the right time Christ died for the ungodly. (Rom. 5:6)

Much more surely then, now that we have been justified by his blood, will we be saved through him from the wrath of God. For if while we were enemies, we were reconciled to God through the death of his Son, much more surely, having been reconciled, will we be saved by his life. (Rom. 5:9–10)

If, because of the one man's trespass, death exercised dominion through that one, much more surely will those who receive the abundance of grace and the free gift of righteousness exercise dominion in life through the one man, Jesus Christ. Therefore just as one man's trespass led to condemnation for all, so one man's act of righteousness leads to justification and life for all. For just as by the one man's disobedience the many were made sinners, so by the one man's obedience the many will be made righteous. But law came in, with the result that the trespass multiplied; but where sin increased, grace abounded all the more. (Rom. 5:17–20)

We find here the foundation for the traditional understanding of Jesus' work of salvation: human beings lost access to God in death, Jesus made access to God possible, and only he could do it.

Augustine's influence further entrenched this thinking. He believed that Adam had the gifts of wonderful knowledge and total mastery of the senses. According to Augustine, Adam, by his sin of pride, became like an animal with the senses out of control. Consequently, passion and inordinate desires ruled him and his offspring. Human knowledge became severely limited. Through Adam's sin, human beings lost the state of paradise and became subject to death.

Humanity, for Augustine, was like a mass of clay, and Adam's sin had caused the clay to deteriorate in quality. Anything made with this clay would now be defective. Furthermore, this defect, the "original sin," was passed on from generation to generation through sexual intercourse. Augustine believed that the passion involved in intercourse was sinful, so every child conceived was born in the devil's power, in actual sin. Jesus, however, was not conceived through sexual intercourse, so he was born without original sin.

The *Catechism of the Catholic Church* provides an excellent example of how this thinking is still enshrined in the Roman Catholic Church's doctrinal framework. It presents the traditional images, language, and beliefs many of us learned at the conventional stage of our faith development:

> Although set by God in a state of rectitude, man, enticed by the evil one, abused his freedom at the very start of history. (no. 415)

> By sin Adam, as the first man, lost the original holiness and justice he had received from God, not only for himself but for all human beings. (no. 416)

> Adam and Eve transmitted to their descendants human nature wounded by their own first sin and hence deprived of original holiness and justice; this deprivation is called "original sin." (no. 417)

> As a result of original sin, human nature is weakened in its powers; subject to ignorance, suffering and the domination of death; and inclined to sin. (This inclination is called "concupiscence.") (no. 418)

> We therefore hold, with the Council of Trent, that original sin is transmitted with human nature, "by propagation, not by imitation" and that it is... "proper to each" (Paul VI, Credo of the People of God, no. 16). (no. 419)

Original sin theology has been at the heart of Christianity's interpretation of Jesus as "savior." This theology was greatly influenced by brilliant thinkers who did not have at their disposal information we have today about the universe and the development of life on earth. Using the information now available to us, we now try to explain the realities of sin, pain, and tragedy. Our information is that the first human beings did not emerge into a state of "original holiness and justice." Far from it. Why, then, should we try to preserve a theological framework clearly dependent on belief in a fall from that state? Why continue to insist that human beings were exiled from God because of a mistake by the first human beings? Do we need to keep telling a story that makes God seem somewhat mean, aloof, punishing, and distant from us? Yes, we can tell that story in a way that reveals God's wonderful mercy, but that story is usually told within the context of exile and banishment. Do we need to rely on a story whose interpretation is so dependent on a dualistic understanding of heaven and the rest of creation?

Today we look around us and see upheavals, disasters, tragedies, and widespread evidence of the human capacity for evil. Like the Hebrews, like Paul, like the early Christian thinkers, we ask where is God in all of this, and what sense can we make of it in the light of a belief that God is good and loving. If we no longer give credence to the belief that the first human beings emerged into a state of paradise, a literal understanding of that story can no longer form the foundation for our questions. In shifting our focus to contemporary knowledge and making this the starting point for our reflection, we may not find perfect answers to all our questions, but at least we are trying to wrestle with the questions within the framework of relevant data.

When Christians move away—as they should—from a literal understanding of the Genesis creation story and move to the new story about the development of life on this planet, they can imagine the reality of God's Spirit at work in a very slow developmental process.

Over billions of years this planet has existed *in* God; over billions of years God's presence was made visible in the unfolding of millions and millions of life forms. God's creative, life-giving Spirit was active billions of years before humankind emerged. We have here a story to capture the mind and the imagination. It is a story capable of moving us to awe, wonder, appreciation, and praise. It is the story of how precious our planet is because, of the multitude of planets, this one just happens to be the right distance from a star capable of sustaining life. It is the story of God's Spirit at work in and through everything on earth—and *life* emerged; and then, with God's Spirit at work, life developed.

We have fossils dating back more than three billion years. Some life forms emerged and died out or were destroyed by other life forms. Death, decay, disaster, and upheavals of enormous proportions were part and parcel of this planet's history long, long before human beings developed to the point where they could add to the damage and disaster. Comets and asteroids bombarded this planet billions of years ago. Dinosaurs appeared, and disappeared more than sixty million years before human beings emerged. The Great Ice Ages also caused widespread destruction of life. Two considerations deserve attention here:

1. Human beings were not responsible for any of this, and

2. God was present in and through it all.

So while we acknowledge the damage human beings have done and are doing to our planet, let us stop blaming human beings as the *initial cause* of decay, disaster, and upheaval on our planet. Let us walk away from a religious imagination that demands we believe human beings emerged into a perfect situation and caused things to go wrong. Let us stop thinking this way.

Instead, let us take seriously the idea of God working in and through what God has to work with. This challenges a popular notion that God could click the divine fingers, as it were, and change the way nature operates. The evidence before our eyes is that God is generally limited by what God has to work with. There are no plants on the moon; no animals on Mars. Human life could not exist on Venus. Pine trees do not grow in Antarctica. God's creative, life-giving presence is limited by and dependent on what the environment presents. Earth's environment is what makes this planet so special: it is just the right distance from a star, has just the right gravitational pull, has an abundance of water thanks to the comets which bombarded it in its early history; it is capable of sustaining life. God's creative, life-giving Spirit is always active on this planet of ours, working in and through what is at hand, and we are blessed with life forms in abundance. However, there are also earthquakes, floods, droughts, famine, volcanic eruptions, and all those other elements that we humans see as imperfections and that cause humanity so much pain. While we would prefer our planet did not operate this way, this is simply reality, the way the universe operates. The upheavals we see on this planet are extremely minor in comparison with the upheavals on other planets or in the midst of stars. It is a very narrow, limited, and erroneous religious imagination that interprets the natural upheavals and upsets we experience on this planet as punishment for an "original sin."

Contemporary knowledge tells us that very, very late in the development of life on earth, after billions of years of a mixture of stunning developments and massive upheavals, human beings emerged. While scientific knowledge concerning human development is sure to increase in the years to come, there is general agreement about the emergence of human-like species from Africa between 500,000 and 34,000 years ago. The Neanderthals were one group (about 135,000 to 34,000 years ago) for which we have the most evidence. They lived in small groups, hunted, used fire and primitive tools, and buried their dead. It is not known whether they had language or the capacity for abstract thinking. They are not considered to be our ancestors. They were more like a "cousin" species to the human species, *homo sapiens,* that emerged and became dominant about the time of the Neanderthals' disappearance. *Homo sapiens,* our direct ancestors, were at one stage as primitive as the Neanderthals, but their capacity for language, abstract thinking, logical thought, and other qualities such as memory, imagination, free will, and love, allowed them to survive and develop.

Scientific evidence suggests that human emergence and development was a slow process. For example, it took thousands of years for human beings to move from the use of crude tools to controlling fire. Early members of the human species were not deeply intelligent, perfectly aware human beings capable of making profound moral choices—least of all a choice that decided the subsequent fate of all of humankind. And if any Christians want to keep insisting that human beings became flawed because of a fall from an original state of paradise, they have to contend with the fact there is no scientific evidence whatever for such an original state. There is no evidence to support the *Catechism of the Catholic Church*'s claim that "because of man, creation is now subject 'to its bondage to decay' " (no. 400).

While this information may undermine the theological framework reliant on taking a "fall" literally, it in no way undermines Christian faith. The theological implications of contemporary knowledge give many Christians a renewed and wonderful sense of God's active presence in the creative process and in the development of life on this planet. They look and see that the emergence of humankind's distinctive intelligence, self-awareness, and consciousness gave God's Spirit a particular way of coming to expression. Of all life forms, human life has the special privilege of conscious awareness of God's creative Spirit at work in all of creation. Because of their special giftedness, human beings not only can give praise and thanks to God, but can be aware of themselves as expressions of the Spirit of God.

When we consider that life started to develop on this planet several *billion* years ago and that mammals and dinosaurs emerged more than two hundred million years ago, the time span of human existence on this planet is a mere blink of the eye in comparison. We are latecomers to this planet. Christians who take this data seriously contemplate the idea of God's creative Spirit working in and through everything on this planet for millions of years before human life emerged. Imagine condensing the history of this planet into a year, and for every moment of that year we thank the Spirit of God for what is emerging. Only on the last day of the year, a few minutes before midnight, would we get to the emergence of human life. Another way of considering how young we humans are on this planet is to imagine a tropical jungle teeming with life and packed with trees of enormous height and width. Imagine a new plant just emerging from the ground, almost totally overwhelmed and awed by the immensity of its surroundings. So much has gone before it. So much has been wonderfully achieved without it. The jungle has brought this fledgling plant into existence and will nurture it and provide for it. It belongs to the jungle; it is *of* the jungle. And even though our particular life form continually prides itself as being superior to all other life forms, it must never lose sight of the fact that the earth and its systems of life brought it into existence. We are *of* the earth, dependent on it for our continued existence.

So where and how did this new life form go wrong? Why is it prone to sin? Why is it so damaging to itself, to the planet, and to the other life forms that nurtured it into existence?

Human beings are not creatures who fell from a perfect state of being. Humans emerged from the earth and its chaos. Humans emerged because of, with, and through the Spirit of God working in the chaos, the imperfection, and the grandeur of planet Earth. Humans emerged and brought with them a host of primeval instincts, emotions, and energies. It is only because we Christians have been totally immersed in a "paradise" story that we feel guilty about and deeply surprised at times by the depth of what we carry within us. We have been led to associate these drives and emotions with sin, but they become "sin" only when we deliberately use them in ways we know we should not.

We should not be surprised that human development, along with the development of social and religious cultures, has been and still is messy, chaotic, and imperfect. As people lived together, bonded, made laws, respected customs, and shaped social interaction and identity, the development of culture put limits on the more primordial human instincts. Aggression and domination had to be balanced with the need of people to live in harmony. The sexual drive had to come to terms with human culture shaping the notion of fidelity to one person. Individual drives such as possessiveness were checked by cultural definition of rights that all people were to enjoy. Society still struggles with these tensions today.

Rather than imagining God's Spirit withdrawing because the first human beings made a terrible mistake, let us imagine the Spirit at the heart of it all. Let us stay with the principle: God's Spirit works in and through what it has to work with. Sin is a reality because human beings have the freedom and the capacity to choose what they know to be wrong. In Christian terms we would name this as a free, deliberate refusal to allow the voice of the "Good Spirit," or conscience or love, to have its way with us. Yet the Spirit is still present. Evil is a reality both because of deliberate sin, but also because of the intrinsic imperfection and struggle of human interactions and relationships. The Spirit is there, but its expression is generally limited by the reality of human behavior. An alcoholic husband who beats his wife and children possesses the Spirit of God, but the Spirit is constrained by all the factors that led the husband to being alcoholic and violent.

We human beings do not sin because something went wrong at the beginning of human history. We sin because the human situation is not perfect and we are free within the reality of that imperfection to make wrong choices. We never lost access to God's Spirit and grace in the struggle to make good choices. We need to be "saved," not in the traditional Christian faith understanding of access to God's presence needing to be restored, but in the sense of needing our eyes and minds to be opened to clear awareness of God's constant presence with us. We will see in the following chapters that the concept of "salvation" will be far richer and more meaningful if we shift the focus from the understanding that Jesus' death restores what was lost to the understanding that Jesus' preaching reveals what always has been. We will also see that our understanding of how God is revealed to us can be enriched by considering revelation in the perspective of the New Story.

Discussion Points

1. What images and thoughts about heaven did you acquire as a young person? What are your images and thoughts now?

2. What do you think will happen to you at death?

3. What was your understanding of original sin? What is your understanding now?

4. What do you think is the source of sin and evil?

Chapter 4

Revelation

THE THEOLOGY OF REVELATION examines how God is revealed to us. It examines how we know who God is, what God is like, and where to look for evidence that God is being revealed to us.

The Hebrew people saw God revealed in their freedom from slavery, in their call to a covenant with God, in the preaching of the prophets, in God's protection and mercy, and in God's punishment of the wicked. They saw the "word" (*dabar*) of God in all these events. *Dabar* means not only the spoken word but also "event or action"—any way God is revealed. Their Scriptures, with the preaching of the prophets and the stories of God's faithfulness to them, was the "word" of God in a special way.

The Christian community continued to understand the "word" of God in this way, but for Christians Jesus of Nazareth was the "word" par excellence: in Jesus, God is revealed in a unique way. In fact, Christians came to believe that Jesus was *the* Word of God, God taking flesh and living among us.

One of the challenges facing Christians, however, is to rescue the understanding of revelation from boundaries that are too narrow, boundaries that have suggested God's revelation was focused on the Hebrew people first, and then, through Jesus, on Christians. Another challenge is to rescue the understanding of revelation from fundamentalism. Fundamentalism is basically a belief that what is recorded in the Scriptures, being divinely inspired, is to be understood as literal truth. Everything described in the pages must have happened exactly as described. Everything written is read as God's "word," as if God had virtually dictated what was written.

This rigid belief took hold at various times and with various groups throughout Christian history. It readily flowed from an understanding that human beings have lived "in exile" from God. In that understanding it was natural to imagine God being elsewhere, breaking into our world from outside it. Revelation came from heaven itself. For fundamentalists, Scripture is God's means of reaching into our world and speaking directly to us.

As we shift from an understanding of living in exile from God to an understanding that God's Spirit has always been and is still active in all of creation, we will inevitably broaden our theology of revelation. We will come to recognize that the whole universe is the primary source of God's revelation. For us, however, this planet holds a special place in that revelation. *Here* we can discern God's presence and God's action in both the world of nature and the world of human interaction. What then becomes obvious is that God's "word" is not confined to any place, culture, or religious group. The boundless energy, dynamism, and creativity of God's Spirit is universal. It recognizes no boundaries. It can be expressed anywhere, anytime.

Our contemporary understanding of revelation should be anchored in the belief that God is present and active everywhere and in all people, at all times. It should also be anchored in the belief that God works in and through what God has to work with. We know the truth of that both from looking at the universe in which we live and from our own experience of family life and our varying personalities. God works in each of us differently and each of us is responsible for the way we allow it to happen.

God's Spirit at work in the Hebrew culture is evident in the preaching of the major prophets. Let us take the prophet Jeremiah as an example. If we want to appreciate the preaching of Jeremiah we have to place him in the historical, political, and religious context of the day, the cultural worldview and the cultural manner of telling stories. It would be helpful also to consider his personality and his background. Then we need to recognize the Spirit of God was at work in all of *this*. The resulting book of Jeremiah was not dictation from heaven. It was the result of the Spirit of God being immersed in and coming to expression in the chaos and the achievements of a particular cultural, social, political, religious, and personal situation. The Scriptures did not drop down from somewhere above. It was here, in the lived situation, that the Spirit was active, seeking to be made manifest.

The Spirit whom we Christians believe "inspires" the Scriptures, does so, but only by working in and through what the Spirit has to work with. If people of a particular time thought the earth was flat and that the sky was a solid vault, then the Spirit of God worked in and through that cultural worldview. However, it does not mean we have to believe the earth is flat or that the sky is a solid vault. Likewise we do not have to believe the creation stories of the Australian aboriginal people or the Native Americans. But we believe the Spirit of God worked in and through the people who shaped these stories and who bore them across the centuries. We believe that their experience of God's Spirit can add insight and depth to our own cultural expressions of God's Spirit at work.

When we read our Scriptures it is important for us to have a sense of the issues stirring in the communities that produced them, for whom they were written, what they believed about the universe, and how they told stories. It is important because these issues, beliefs, and ways of telling stories are the elements in which and by which the presence of God's Spirit is manifested. This is true for both the Old and the New Testaments. The Scriptures are documents written by people of faith communities at a particular time in history, immersed in their own particular problems and their own religious, cultural worldview, trying to make sense of their relationship with God. Our task, in reading them, is not to get caught up in the historically and culturally conditioned factors of the time, but to engage and learn from their insights about God and human existence that transcend such conditioning. If we adopt a fundamentalist approach to Scripture, we risk being sidetracked by the recorded details, events, customs, laws, and worldviews that are not essential to ongoing belief. We might then go overboard and claim that these human constructions *are* essential to belief and must be adhered to.

If the Spirit of God works in and through the development of culture, we would expect to find a development of religious insight as culture develops. This is just what we do find. The Hebrew Scriptures clearly show a development of insight and belief with regard to some key issues. This is an indication of the Spirit of God working within the confines of increasing human knowledge along with human reflection on life. For example, the belief in *one God* took a long time to take a firm hold in the minds and religious practice of the Hebrew people. The idea of life after death is another example. The idea was virtually unknown for centuries, and at the time of Jesus was still a point of debate between the Sadducees and the Pharisees. We can look to the Psalms for another instance of development of insight and belief. It was proclaimed that the wicked will suffer and the good person will prosper, and that for whoever takes delight in the Law of Yahweh everything undertaken will turn out well (see Ps. 1; 58:11; and 37:25). Doubtless people tried to live in this faith and doubtless many found over the years that reflection on their own experience of life caused them to question these statements, even though the statements belong to the "word" of God.

Revelation unfolded within and through human experience, reflection, and increasing knowledge. We need to recognize that it was not confined to one religious culture. God's Spirit was at work in the Chinese culture, the Indian cultures, and in all other cultures at the same time God's Spirit was at work in the Hebrew people. The Scriptures of other religions are as much expressions of God's Spirit leading people to wisdom and insight as are our Scriptures. They, too, are the "word" of God. When we recognize this, we come to a greater appreciation of how revelation works and how universal it is. Christians moving into adult stages of faith development are coming to appreciate this more and more and are increasingly open to discovering religious truth and insight beyond the cultural confines of Judaism and Christianity. However, people whose faith is stalled at the conventional stage of development are suspicious of this movement. To them it seems a betrayal of the uniqueness of Christianity and its Scripture.

Rather than a betrayal, it should be seen as a necessary part of our present-day effort to encounter God revealed in the life and teaching of Jesus. We cannot and should not be trying to encounter our basic Christian story without taking into consideration that God's Spirit is active everywhere. This consideration will influence the way we hear and tell the story of Jesus today. It will influence how we answer the perennial questions about Jesus: How does Jesus "reveal" God to us? Who is Jesus? How does Jesus "save" us?

Traditional Christian faith maintains that Jesus is the definitive revelation of God; he saved us from the dire consequences of the "fall"; he restored access to God's glory to us; he ensured God's forgiveness for our sins. In accomplishing

all this he had to be more than human because no human
person could do these things.

St. Athanasius, preaching and writing in the fourth century,
further developed the church's classical theological understanding of "salvation" and shaped the church's language and
ideas about Jesus in relationship with God within this understanding. Like Paul, he thought in terms of Adam's sin cutting
off the possibility of eternal life with God. He argued that only
God could restore human beings to communion with Himself,
and that if Jesus were less than an actual incarnation of God,
then we could not be "saved." Athanasius wrote:

> What else could He possibly do, being God, but renew
> His Image in mankind, so that through it men might
> once more come to know Him? And how could this be
> done save by the coming of the very Image Himself, our
> Savior Jesus Christ? Men could not have done it, for they
> are only made after the Image; nor could the angels have
> done it, for they are not the images of God. The Word of
> God came in His own Person, because it was He alone,
> the Image of the Father, Who could recreate man made
> after the Image. . . .
>
> Now that the common Savior of all has died on our
> behalf, we who believe in Christ no longer die, as men
> died aforetime, in fulfillment of the threat of the law.
> That condemnation has come to an end; and now by the
> grace of the resurrection, corruption has been banished
> and done away with, we are loosed from our mortal bod-
> ies in God's good time for each, so that we may obtain
> thereby a better resurrection. . . .
>
> The Lord came to overthrow the devil and to purify
> the air and to make "a way" for us up to heaven. . . .

Athanasius highlighted the prevailing religious imagination
that Jesus had to be more on God's side than the rest of hu-

manity for salvation to be achieved. Humankind could not restore within itself the "image of God." Humankind could not gain entrance into heaven of its own accord. However, this created dilemmas for Christian thinkers. If Jesus is "the image of the Father" was he really *human?* And isn't there just *one* God, so how can Jesus be identified with God? If he is indeed to be named as "true God and true man" what language can be found to express what seems to be a contradiction of ideas? Gradually, after much argument and dissent, Christianity came to define, especially in the Councils of Nicaea and Chalcedon (fourth and fifth centuries), in technical language its belief that Jesus had both a divine and a human nature and that these existed in the one person. It defined and enshrined in its Creed the belief that there are three "persons" in the one God. It defined the belief that the second person was "begotten of" and "one in substance with" the first, and that the third "proceeded" from the first and the second, while all three are equal.

In addition to the teaching of Jesus and the way it reveals God as a God of love and a God of mercy present with us in human interactions, the Christian church now had answers to the dilemmas posed by their understanding of Jesus' role in salvation. The questions were encased in doctrinal formulations with precise and technical language. Who is Jesus? Jesus is the incarnation of the Second Person of the Trinity; he is the divine Savior of the entire human race; he is "true God and true man." What did Jesus reveal about God apart from God being loving and merciful? Jesus revealed that God is a Trinity of Persons. What did Jesus achieve? Jesus achieved reconciliation with God, access to God's glory, and the assurance of the forgiveness of our sins.

Thereafter, Christian theology proceeded on the understanding that one cannot be an orthodox, right-thinking, Christian theologian without operating within the boundaries of these defined teachings. Theology may speculate how we might better understand these doctrines today, but is not permitted to question them. Most Christians have been taught these doctrines and taught also not to question them.

Yet it is clear today that many Christians, in the normal process of adult faith development, especially as they engage elements of the New Story with the conviction that God's Spirit is active everywhere, *are* asking questions. They are disturbed that the faith they were taught rests so strongly on underlying premises people at the beginning of the twenty-first century find hard to accept. They find the language and concepts of the Nicaean Creed irrelevant to their lives. They are committed Christians, but want their faith articulated and expressed in concepts and language which respect the realities of these times.

These Christians, immersed in the belief that creation is and always has been permeated with God's presence and that God's Spirit is constantly being revealed in our midst, see no need for a god-figure to come down from heaven and restore us to God's friendship and presence. They have a different understanding, as we shall see in the next chapter, of how Jesus reveals what God is like and how God is connected with all human beings.

If our starting point is God who is always present and active in creation, then revelation and salvation will not be concerned with regaining what was never lost. Salvation will be concerned with identifying God's presence and allowing it to have expression in our lives. We will not see ourselves as "poor, banished children of Eve," exiled from God. Rather, we will want to acknowledge the wonder of who we are and God's constant presence with us as we grapple with the fact that we can be ungrateful, unreflective, selfish, cruel, proud, stubborn, and all the other things that make sin and evil visible among us. We humans have so much going for us; yet we act toward each other and toward this planet as if the Spirit of God were not present and active in all of creation and in us. The Spirit works in and through us, but it is as if we put the Spirit in a straitjacket and allow ourselves to be moved only so far by the Spirit's promptings. What we need desperately is someone to light the way of human existence for us, to show us how the Spirit of God may be better expressed in our lives, how to create a human society that will give witness to God's "reign" among us. For us Christians it is Jesus to whom we look in order to free ourselves from the hold of sin and evil. It is by contemplating his life and his preaching that we see the real point of human existence. In him we see how God's Spirit might be given proper expression in us.

Discussion Points

1. What has been your understanding of revelation and the way it happens?

2. Were you ever literalist in your reading of Scripture? Who or what helped you to read Scripture differently?

3. What scriptural story, event, or passage has taken on new meaning or significance for you because of a better understanding of its background or formation?

4. What do you understand "salvation" to mean and what role does Jesus play in it?

– *Chapter 5* –

The Teaching of Jesus

EXAMINING THE BASIC INSIGHTS of Jesus of Nazareth within the framework of the New Story rather than within the framework of the fall-redemption story presents a massive shift for Christian theology.

This attempt at the task is not motivated by a desire to dismiss doctrinal formulations based on the fall-redemption story. Rather, the task is attempted with the conviction that if the people who shaped those traditional formulations were alive today, they would certainly use the knowledge and information of this age to articulate their understanding of Jesus.

The task is to understand Jesus and his message in the context of the Spirit of God being actively present in all places at all times in a universe that has existed for at least twelve billion years.

Can we consider Jesus in the context of contemporary knowledge about the universe and our planet? Can we move our understanding of Jesus beyond the framework of a particular story of creation and a fall that was shaped in a completely different cosmology?

Can we try to imagine the Spirit of God coming to expression, in great bursts of wisdom and insight, not only within the Jewish religion but also in other religions around the world? Can we imagine this constant, global phenomenon of God's revelation operating and coming to expression in whatever God has to work with?

Can we imagine the Spirit of God coming to expression in Jesus of Nazareth in the context of the Spirit prompting people all over the world—for thousands of years before Jesus was born—to ask questions about the purpose of life, to explore interest in the sacred dimension of life, to ask what connection there might be between a God, gods, or spirits and human beings?

Can we do our imagining with the conviction that there is one God, one Spirit, yet many cultural and religious expressions that give God different names, different understandings, different formulations of belief, different institutional systems of religion?

Can we examine the teaching of Jesus as people who believe that in him the Spirit of God came to its clearest, most wonderful human expression?

And can we then, in a global context, articulate what it is in the message and life of this man that offers insight and good news to the questions human beings ask about life and its connectedness to the realm of the sacred?

So we consider the life and preaching of Jesus, conscious we are doing so in a selective way. We look to see how the Spirit moved in him and speaks to all of us through him.

At a point relatively late in his adult life, Jesus of Nazareth became a "man with a mission." The stories of his baptism which herald his public entry into this mission are stories of a man prepared to give his heart and soul, his "very all," as the great commandment of love expresses it, to allow God's Spirit to move him completely. Luke's Gospel links the story of the baptism of Jesus with the story of him being driven by the Spirit of God. "Jesus, full of the Holy Spirit, returned from the Jordan" and went into the wilderness (Luke 4:1). "Jesus, filled with the power of the Spirit, returned to Galilee"(Luke

4:14). Jesus' first public proclamation in Luke's Gospel took place in Nazareth, and it began with Jesus citing the prophet Isaiah: "The Spirit of the Lord is upon me" (4:18). Filled with the Spirit and committed to giving his life to the promptings of the Spirit, Jesus moved around the countryside preaching.

Many Christians when asked what message it was that Jesus preached give bland responses: he preached "love," he preached "forgiveness," he preached "a loving God," and so on. And that's true. But such responses do not do justice to Jesus or his preaching nor are they persuasive for people looking to see if Christianity has a worthwhile message to offer. If the Christian religion has something worthwhile to say to a contemporary world that is fast becoming more and more dismissive of many of Christianity's traditional theological images, language, and claims, this "something worthwhile" has to be and will be found in the preaching of Jesus. And Christians must be able to articulate it with clarity and enthusiasm.

Jesus' preaching reflected his basic religious convictions. He believed that his understanding of and insights about God and life would be good news for people. Quoting Isaiah, he shared his conviction that his preaching would be "good news to the poor," would bring freedom to those who were "captive," bring sight to those who were "blind," and "set the down-trodden free." By his words and actions he tried to show how and why his message was good news.

What seems most universally applicable about Jesus' message was his conviction that the "reign of God" or "the kingdom of God" was at hand. He called people to conversion so that they might believe this good news. He believed that many of his contemporaries were beset with wrong ideas about God and were looking for their experience of God in the wrong place. He recognized some of the biggest obstacles to conversion were ingrained ideas and images which prevented people from believing that God was close to them and which led them to be fearful of God. Again and again, in preaching about the "reign of God" and in sharing his conviction that God was not to be feared, Jesus tried to undermine these barriers to believing the good news he wanted to share.

How are people to recognize that the reign, kingdom, or rule of God is in their midst? Jesus made clear that there were clear, unmistakable signs: when people act or see others act in ways that are good, truthful, loving, forgiving, just, and merciful they should realize these are the signs of God's Spirit present and active in human interactions. Jesus urged people to see the connection: live in love and you live in God. He identified, and wanted them to identify, basic human interactions such as visiting one another, clothing the poor, caring for the needy, being ready to forgive, feeding children, overcoming cultural prejudices, respecting women, loving one's neighbor as oneself, and being wholeheartedly generous as the "rule" of God. Here is where all people would be able to recognize and name the presence of God's Spirit in their midst.

Jesus preached that the "poor in spirit" have a special insight into God's reign. He most likely experienced a capacity for generosity and sharing among the poor in Nazareth, an experience that deepened his conviction that the kingdom of God "belonged" to the poor in a special way.

Jesus made it clear that there was no easy path to ushering in God's reign. It demands purity of heart, a commitment to peace, readiness to forgive, generosity, the endurance of persecution and calumny, truly being neighbor to those in need, renouncing self, being ready to take the hard road. The job description calls for large, loving, generous hearts.

The pure in heart shall "see" God. Do we understand this in a future sense only? Would it not be legitimate to understand this "seeing" in the here and now? Obviously, we are not referring here to a literal "seeing" of God, but trying to

engage and share the heart of Jesus' insight: when you are
like this, when you do this, you will experience God's Spirit
working in and through you. Christians and non-Christians
alike are able to recognize the goodness in human encoun-
ters. Loving behavior is a universal phenomenon. We could
explore with people who are pure in heart, Christians and
non-Christians, whether the way they live life is accompanied
with an awareness of a sacred dimension of life. Not everyone who is pure in heart will want to make the transition into
religious or spiritual language, but the many who do will find
in the teaching of Jesus a shared conviction that transcends
the doctrinal boundaries of particular religions.

Two issues have particular importance here. One is the
need for religious language that reflects the presence of the
one Spirit of God working in all people. The other is the need
of religion generally to have its claims to "truth" about the
sacred validated by universal human experience. We need religious dialogue that is not sidetracked by claims of "truth"
that are dependent on a particular cultural worldview or
by claims to be exclusive bearers of God's revelation to
the world.

The teaching of Jesus has much to offer in this movement to
a broader, more inclusive conversation about how and where
God is revealed and how God can be encountered.

For Jesus, peacemakers are "sons and daughters" of God.
He taught that people who give to those who ask, who pray
for those who persecute them are also "sons and daughters
of your Father in heaven" (Matt. 5:45).

Being a "son or daughter of God" is not identified here
with membership of a particular religious or cultural group.
It is far more universal in its identification and application.
Anyone who acts like this is showing that they are living and
acting as a son or daughter of God. Anyone.

Surely this statement does not rely on belonging to any

particular religious or cultural group. It is a statement about anyone who is generous.

Are we sufficiently aware of what Jesus was doing in his preaching?

On the one hand, he was laying down an imperative: if you want to discover God's presence in your life, be a peacemaker, forgive, be generous, be compassionate. There is no other way.

On the other hand, Jesus was trying to help people who actually live this way to name and be aware of God's Spirit active in their actions.

For Jesus, the presence of God's Spirit is evident in human interactions of mercy, compassion, forgiveness, sharing, working for justice, respect, joy, working for peace. When you see these things, you *know* God's Spirit is here. When you do these things, you *know* God's Spirit is here in you. Jesus called people to *recognize and name* the active presence of God's Spirit in their midst.

This should be the heart of the Gospel message Christianity shares with the world today. The good news is that in everyday, decent human interaction all people encounter the sacred, the Spirit of God at work. All people, not just Christians, are people in and through whom the Spirit acts so that God's "rule" might be established. All people are "God's people." This is a Wow! statement about human existence, about who we are, what we all share and where we encounter God and the "sacred." If we believed this good news, we would look at ourselves, other people, human interaction, and all of creation differently.

The urgency in Jesus' teaching is clear: this is what life is about. Be alert; seize the opportunity and the challenge. We are to "set our hearts on the kingdom first" and so build our "houses" on rock. If we do this we will be like people who have discovered a treasure in a field. Part of the treasure we discover will be an answer to the anxiety that has plagued many religions and many religious people: are we to fear God?

If our actions of decent human living are visible expressions of God's presence among us, how can we fear God? There is no place for fear here. If we are fearful, our images of and ideas about God need changing. So Jesus, by his use of images and parables, calls us to conversion in the way we think and act, wanting us to be "set free" from images, ideas, and religious practices that bind and enslave us into fear of God rather than help us embrace God's presence in our lives.

Throughout human history people have asked: Where is God? Is God a distant overseer figure, looking down on us? Jesus invites us into the conviction that God is intimately *near* us, intimately connected with our own loving. The consequences of looking to encounter a distant God rather than encountering a God with us are enormous. Why pray, for example, to a distant God to care for the downtrodden when God's concern and care for the downtrodden is dependent on our compassion and generosity for expression? Hope for the downtrodden lies in God's "sons and daughters" accepting the responsibility of establishing God's rule in our world. Hope lies in people willing to believe that their political, commercial, moral, and social choices give expression to God's Spirit at work in this world.

Considered in the context of the universality of Jesus' teaching, "salvation" is being set free from images, ideas, and practices that bind us into enslavement to a distant, overseer God, being set free from fear of God, being set free from divisions that divide people and set them against each other in the name of religion and being set free from thinking and acting as if we had no personal authority to promote justice, truth, and the action of God's Spirit in our world. This understanding challenges all of us to take responsibility for the emergence of God's reign. It is a significant shift from understanding salvation in terms of Jesus regaining access to God's glory for us. God's reign is still to emerge; salvation is still to happen for many, many people—and the responsibility rests squarely on our shoulders if we are to be true disciples of Jesus.

Some Christians want to question this concept of "salvation." After all, doesn't the term traditionally refer to Jesus "saving us" and getting us into heaven?

Yes, the term has traditionally been used with that understanding. However, it is clear in the Gospels that Jesus did not relate with people on that basis. Nor did his teaching about the reign of God in our midst reflect such an understanding. On the contrary, the Gospels indicate:

- Jesus did not relate with the poor and the sinners on the understanding that God was distant from them.

- Jesus did not relate with the poor and the sinners on the understanding that God's forgiveness had been and was being withheld from them.

- Jesus never indicated any understanding whatever of the traditional "original sin" theology which held that all human beings are born in a state of separation from God's grace. The notion of people being blocked from access to God's loving presence is contrary to the heart of Jesus' teaching.

- Jesus did not relate with people on the understanding that he was the dispenser, the mediator of God's presence for them. On the contrary, he urged people to reflect on their own lived experience and through their reflection to grow in awareness and in confidence of God's presence with them.

What stands out in the life of Jesus is that he practiced what he preached. In him people recognized God's Spirit at work. Here, clearly, was a peacemaker, someone pure of heart, humble in spirit, generous, forgiving, a man of great love for and service to others. Here was a true "son" of God. The extraordinary impact of Jesus' actions and preaching on his followers moved them to articulate their basic religious conviction about life and God.

The foundational religious insight and conviction of Christianity became: *when we live in love, we live in God and God lives in us.* In an age of disbelief and cynicism this is the spiritual conviction Christianity could and should be promoting as hope for the world. This could be common ground with all people and as such could form the basis of religious dialogue.

This dialogue would not be attempting to make the whole world Christian or to forge one world religion. Rather, it would be seeking a common ground in religious insights that could be of benefit to human interaction. Of course we will find that our word "God" will not be used universally. All sorts of names (or even the refusal to put any name on what we Christians try to point to with our word "God") will be used by people in other places and cultures. But collectively, as human beings of all religious persuasions trying to engage this great Mystery, we can and should examine *together* whether there is validity in believing that human loving enables us to encounter this Mystery. And if collectively human beings worked together sharing this belief, it would make an enormous contribution to human existence. Respect, sharing, care, concern, openness, and genuinely being neighbor to one another might emerge more on a world scale in place of suspicion, religious fanaticism, and wars generated by centuries of religious bigotry and hatred and exclusive claims to "the truth" by any one religion.

Is this dreaming? It may well be, but as Christians let us be utterly clear and convinced this was the dream of Jesus of Nazareth when he preached about God's reign being seen on this earth.

The Christian religion has in the preaching of Jesus a "universal" message of salvation to share with the world. It is this, rather than traditional concepts and doctrinal teaching about "salvation" that stressed access to eternal life being dependent on Jesus, that will enhance and promote widespread belief that all people are God's people.

If we look at what we Christians consider to be the "birth" of our religion, Pentecost, we will find this "universal" message of salvation grounded, as it was in Jesus' preaching, in the experience of people being set free from fear and in their conviction that they shared the powerful presence of God's Spirit in their lives.

There were two key elements in the Pentecost experience. Both were essential, for without either one of them, Christianity would never have left Jerusalem.

First, a group of people came to recognize that Jesus whom they had known so well and whom they had let down so badly had lived totally a life of love and readiness to forgive. They believed that the God about whom Jesus had preached raised Jesus from the dead into God's presence, where he "received from the Father the promise of the Holy Spirit" (Acts 2:33) and now became their "Lord and Messiah" (Acts 2:36). Reflection on Jesus' life and his message led them to recognize that he had indeed lived in love, lived in God, and *God had lived in him.* These words are so familiar to us that we can fail to appreciate their depth and significance. These people came to believe that in the human life they had been privileged to know for several years they had come to a deeper understanding of what God is like. They now stood convinced that God is love. It was the life of a human person that finally convinced them.

We Christians would do well to contemplate and ponder what happened here. A human person was so able to live human life that other people reflecting on his life came to a rich understanding of what God is like.

Reflection on Jesus' life can lead us to reflect further on human life in general and our own lives in particular. Could it be true for all of us, if we too lived lives steeped in love, that people contemplating our lives could have a richer understanding of what God is like? This leads to the second significant element of Pentecost.

In the Pentecost experience, however it took place, the followers of Jesus came to a,clear belief and awareness that the same Spirit they had seen in Jesus was present and active in their lives. They came to believe that this Spirit could be as courageously expressed in their lives as Jesus had allowed it to be in his life.

Was the presence of the Spirit of God in their lives a new phenomenon conferred only by Jesus returning to heaven and "sending" the Spirit? The scriptural story of Pentecost makes it appear they received a gift they had not formerly possessed. John's Gospel presents the belief that unless Jesus returned to the Father the Spirit would not come down to earth. Christian tradition continued to present an understanding that the return of Jesus to heaven opened the way for the Spirit to come upon the followers of Jesus and all who are baptized.

We can continue to understand the experience of Pentecost as the granting of the Spirit in a special way or we can understand it in the belief that God's Spirit has never been absent from any aspect of creation. In this understanding Jesus did not send the Spirit. No, his life and death led his followers to the realization that they shared the same Spirit he had and they were now being challenged by that awareness to witness to the Spirit in their lives as courageously as Jesus did.

Only when Jesus' followers came to this religious insight and conviction—to which Jesus had tried without success to move them—and determined to act upon it did the Christian missionary movement begin in Jerusalem. And the message of "good news" preached to the world was the story of Jesus, the human person who revealed the divine and who revealed to all of us the wonder of who we are.

Who are we? The New Testament writers answered this question in beautiful images. We are earthen vessels that hold a treasure, God's work of art, temples of God's Spirit, the body of Christ, God's sons and daughters.

If we Christians, like Jesus, lived and preached this understanding, the reign of God would indeed be seen among us and Christianity would have something of great value to share and explore with people searching for the meaning of human existence. If all people on earth shared and bonded together in similar convictions about the sacredness of human life, the world would indeed be a better place.

It is this understanding of who human beings are that constitutes the foundations of a Christian "spirituality." We attend to the story of Jesus because this story reveals not only God but also our capacity as human beings to give expression to God's Spirit. We use the teaching and story of Jesus to articulate our understanding of life and who we are. We live with a belief and with a sense that we are "Spirit" people, "sons and daughters" of God, temples of God's Spirit. This belief is at the heart of Christian prayer in which we constantly give thanks to God and also seek to deepen our awareness of God's Spirit active in and through us. It identifies our loving and "being there" for our neighbor, individually and on a global scale, as God's way of being there. If this spirituality is not clearly articulated, promoted, ritualized and manifested, then the Christian church risks being crippled because of its failure to present a wholesome understanding of human beings in relationship with God.

How is this spirituality manifested? Again, we only have to look at the life of Jesus for guidance. Jesus allowed the Spirit of God to motivate his life completely. In him we find someone who pitched his tent with the poor, the lowly, and the sinners, not the high, the mighty, the powerful, and the righteous. We find someone who lived in service to others and did so with extraordinary patience and compassion. Here was a man who broke cultural and ethnic boundaries and scandalized leaders of his own society. He was equally at home with outcasts, with fishermen, with religious leaders, with women, with preaching in the market place, and with retiring to a private space to reflect.

All of this impinges on our understanding of "salvation." For what Jesus did was to show how we might set one another free in the here and now. Serve one another; break down boundaries; affirm one another; treat one another as equals; share with one another; forgive one another; challenge one another; be with one another; listen to one another; and show you understand the longings of one another's hearts. Be neighbor to one another rather than ask who your neighbor is. This is what will set the Spirit of God free in our midst. This is what will make the world a better place.

One thing Jesus did not do was to formulate doctrinal propositions and hold these up as a test of whether people were "in" or "out," "right" or "wrong." No, he preached and lived a "Spirit," and his preaching and his living challenge Christians to do the same. This is how God's "salvation" will be known in our world. This is what the "reign of God" is about. This is where we are to know, experience, and build up the "kingdom of God." And if we are to formulate doctrinal propositions and set up church authority to safeguard them, each must be based on the teaching and example of Jesus. Doctrine and the exercise of authority must always be servants of the Spirit. Such an approach would allow the Spirit—and spirituality—room to move and expand, erupting in new and surprising ways. It might help us to adapt, to be refreshed and energized. Then, and only then, will the Spirit have much chance to "renew the face of the earth." Our prayer for the Spirit to do so might be prayed with a vitality that echoes the enthusiasm of Pentecost.

Discussion Points

1. In your adult years have you found that a renewed understanding of Jesus' teaching has significantly altered your religious thinking, imagination, or practice?

2. Articulate what you believe to be the basics of a wholesome Christian spirituality.

– Chapter 6 –

God Raised Jesus

CHRISTIANS BELIEVE in the resurrection of Jesus. We believe that God "raised" Jesus from death. We are not sure what "raised" entails since we do not know what actually happened. We believe Jesus died and that his dead body was laid to rest. The dead body did not come back to life again and resume human existence as Jesus had experienced it before death, whatever Gospel stories of the risen Jesus eating with and being touched by people might suggest. The reality is we simply do not know anything more about how God raised Jesus from the dead than we know about how God has raised our deceased relatives and friends from the dead. We know they are not in their graves. We believe they are now "in" God, "raised into God," and we know very little about this dimension of existence. Perhaps the greatest mystery about human life is what happens beyond our present mode of existence. It is so mysterious and unknown that human imagination dealing with life beyond the grave has grappled with language and images, some more helpful than others. When we reflect on the resurrection of Jesus, our first step is to clear away some of the ideas and images that prevail in popular thought and imagination.

It is very hard to let go of images and ideas into which we have been nurtured and which have been a comfort to us in facing the unknown. The reality we have to face, though, is that many of our images and ideas about life after death depend on a dualistic worldview. How many of us have been nurtured in the thinking that life is a journey to God? We live here. We die. Then we, our "souls," go somewhere else. It is like a journey away from here, a journey to "heaven." What have we imagined? A floating "up" and a looking down? Isn't it a fact that most of us Christians have been steeped in the imagination that death brings a journey to somewhere beyond this earth, way, way beyond? Yet there is no way, way beyond in this universe of ours. Just millions of galaxies beyond millions of galaxies, beyond millions of galaxies.

So let us be clear that death does not entail a journey for the soul to a place somewhere else. No, death is an entrance into a new mode of existence. It is not a physical existence. It is a new way of existing "in" God, different from the physical way we now exist "in" God. And the very fact that we Christians believe we are now living in God leads us to believe we are already participating in eternal life.

The notions of heaven as a place, somewhere else, where God exists, separation between heaven and earth, death as a journey to somewhere beyond earth, and judgment deciding who will or will not gain entry belong to a dualistic worldview. We need to decide, then, at the beginning of any reflection on the resurrection of Jesus whether it is in that worldview that we will continue to interpret the importance of Jesus' resurrection.

In traditional Christian thinking, the entire human race lost access to heaven through the fault of the first human beings. Before Jesus every human being who lived a good life went at death to "hell," not the hell of eternal damnation, but the "hell" of the Creed: "he descended into hell." This hell was a limbo, a holding place for good people waiting for the coming of the Savior who would open the gates of heaven to them. Jesus by his manner of living and dying restored access to eternal life with God and assured us of God's forgiveness and a place in heaven after death. Furthermore, only by being significantly different from us—by being actually God—could Jesus by his life and death effect this change.

Another intrinsic aspect of the traditional understanding of Jesus' resurrection from the dead is that the sending of God's Spirit upon humanity was dependent on Jesus' return to heaven, the ascension.

We find these elements in the *Catechism of the Catholic Church* in its statements concerning the ascension of Jesus:

> The final stage stays closely linked to the first, that is, to his descent from heaven in the Incarnation. Only the one who "came from the Father" can return to the Father: Christ Jesus. "No one has ascended into heaven but he who descended from heaven, the Son of man" (Jn 3:13). Left to its own natural powers humanity does not have access to the "Father's house," to God's life and happiness. Only Christ can open to man such access that we, his members, might have confidence that we too shall go where he, our Head and our Source, has preceded us. (no. 661)

> Jesus Christ, having entered the sanctuary of heaven once and for all, intercedes constantly for us as the mediator who assures us of the permanent outpouring of the Holy Spirit. (no. 667)

Many of us have had our Christian faith nurtured and developed in this doctrinal framework and its images. It is a huge step for any of us to question the scenario, let alone to say quite clearly to ourselves and maybe to others: "I just do not believe this any more." It is not belief in the resurrection being rejected. It is not the message of Jesus being rejected. It is not a rejection of desiring to live life as a person inspired by the life, death, rising, and teaching of Jesus. It is not a rejection of Jesus being uniquely a revelation of God's presence. It is not a rejection of Christianity. It is none of these things. It is, instead, a firm desire to rescue the liberating person, Jesus, and his teaching from a worldview that makes no sense to us. How can people with an understanding of the universe being thoroughly immersed *in* God's loving presence, "charged" with God's creative Spirit, take seriously images of "descending" from and "ascending" to "heaven"? How can we take seriously the belief that only through Jesus is access to God's "life and happiness" possible? How can we take seriously the belief that humanity "left to its own natural powers" does not have access to "the Father's house" when the heart of Jesus' message proclaimed that living in love is living in God and God living in us? How can we take seriously the notion of Jesus being necessary as a "mediator" to "ensure" the constant outpouring of the Holy Spirit when we believe the universe itself is a manifestation of the constant presence of that Spirit?

We can firmly believe in the resurrection of Jesus. We can firmly believe God raised Jesus into the mystery of life beyond death. But let us free our understanding and appreciation from connotations of Jesus switching something back on or winning back something humankind had lost.

Let us instead consider the resurrection of Jesus in the belief that all human persons who lived before Jesus and who died with an orientation to love in their hearts died *in* God, and died *into* the mystery of life beyond human existence. As Christians we are guided by the insights of Jesus, who firmly believed that in death we meet a God, loving, compassionate, and generous beyond our imagining.

Another way of expressing this belief is to assert that God has *always* raised, has never stopped raising, human beings into the mystery of eternal life beyond this present mode of existence. Isaiah was raised by God; Confucius was raised by God; Buddha was raised by God; Zoroaster was raised by God. These great religious leaders might reject the Christian language and understanding of resurrection. However, it is important for our contemporary Christian perspective that we speak inclusively and universally, trying to take seriously that it is one and the same Spirit of God at work in all places. That Spirit, at work in all places at all times, offered to people in all places at all times the possibility of eternal life with God. Jesus did not regain it, for it was never lost.

This understanding is radically different from the under-standing that permeates the New Testament Scriptures and the tradition of the Christian church. Christianity is indeed at a crossroads at this point of history. Will it keep walking down the dualistic road with the images we saw above from the *Catechism of the Catholic Church?* Or will it step into the twenty-first century and begin the massive task of reformu-lating its understanding of the life, death, and rising of Jesus within the framework of contemporary knowledge?

What might happen to our understanding and appreciation of the resurrection of Jesus if we do make this shift?

The answer lies in who Jesus is for us and what he preached. Jesus lived and died in total openness to love. He urged people to name their loving as a sharing in God's Spirit and the means by which God's reign would be established in human society. He urged people to trust rather than to fear God. He urged people to believe in a compassionate, faithful God. He was firmly convinced that openness to love is open-ness to God encountered in love and that you could not have one without the other. The first Christians believed they saw all of this epitomized in the life of Jesus. He gave all he had for the reign of God. He was a man who defined the very meaning and purpose of human existence by linking human love with divine love.

If Jesus was not raised by God, then everything Jesus lived and died for loses all credibility. We would not believe that human love and divine love are intrinsically connected; we would not believe that loving God and neighbor go hand in hand; we would not believe that living in love is to experience living in God and God living in us and that there is an eternal dimension to our living in God. We would not be convinced that God is faithful. There would be no solid foundation to trust rather than to fear God.

The life, teaching, and resurrection of Jesus led people to convictions about life, death, God, and themselves that formed the foundations of a new "faith." People saw in Jesus God made visible. They came to believe that if they too lived in love they too would be living in God and God in them. They believed there is an eternal dimension to this, that love would survive beyond the grave. These beliefs set their hearts on fire, freed them from fear, superstition, and dependence on ritual legalism, and motivated them to spread this "good news." The message that God had raised Jesus vindicated everything Jesus had lived and preached.

Yes, God raised Jesus. That's our faith. But he was not the first, nor is he the one who made life after death and access to eternal life with God *possible*. His life and preaching made it possible for people to see clearly and to appreciate the richness of human existence and how human love is interwoven with God and God's reign on this planet. Christians came to understand that this man's life was like a mirror to them, revealing the ultimate purpose in life: living in love is intrinsically connected with being raised in death into eternal life with God.

As we begin a new millennium we Christians want our hearts to be set on fire by the story of the life, death, and rising of Jesus. Some Christians will have their hearts set on fire by traditional thought patterns and images. Many others—and the number seems to be increasing rapidly—realize the story needs to be told in a completely new and contemporary way. A key issue in the way we tell the story of Jesus' resurrection is whether we tell the story in the belief that no one was raised into eternal life with God before Jesus lived and died.

This is one example of where institutionalized religion will not support any movement away from the traditional interpretation. Yet many adult Christians, influenced by the new story about our cosmos and how God's Spirit has always been present and active, have already moved in their thinking.

It would be healthy and helpful if we Christians could discuss the resurrection of Jesus more openly. We need to examine what images and ideas have influenced and now influence our beliefs, to share why we believe what we believe, and to engage the issues that will inevitably arise in the discussion. It would be healthy and helpful if leadership in our respective churches were to discuss with us at this level of crucial and critical examination. It would also be healthy and helpful to have access to church scholarship not bound by threats of silencing and condemnation if it stretched our minds and our thinking on issues such as this.

Consider, for example, belief in the *physical* resurrection of Jesus.

The Gospel stories about an empty tomb have been at the forefront of discussion about the manner of Jesus' resurrection. These stories have to be understood as an attempt to deal with the great mystery of life after death. Jesus is dead, yes, but he is alive. Jesus is gone, yes, but he is still here with us.

It is significant that Paul never mentions the physical resurrection of Jesus. For Paul, the most important aspect of the resurrection of Jesus was that God raised the human person Jesus into God's "glory," into the fullest possible reception of God's Spirit. In Paul's understanding this made it possible for us to receive and be bathed in that same "glory"—so we, through Jesus, became sons and daughters of God also, "co-heirs" with Jesus. We became "temples of God's Spirit." This is why Paul pronounced that Christianity is worthless without the resurrection.

Paul was not concerned *how* the resurrection happened. His focus was on its effects.

Influenced by the Gospels, many of us have been accustomed to understanding the resurrection differently. The Gospels, written another generation after Paul, carry stories of an empty tomb. These stories were recorded to support the already established and firm belief in the resurrection of Jesus. They deal with the mystery and wonder of yes, but.... Yes, he died, but.... Yes, he has gone, but.... However, when the Christian tradition and popular imagination interpreted the stories of a physical body moving through walls or eating breakfast on the beach in a literal way, the physicality of the resurrection was understood to be factual.

Emphasis on the empty tomb and the physical appearances caused these elements to be considered "facts" on which the truth of Jesus' resurrection relied. For many Christians these "factual" elements proved both that God had raised Jesus and that Jesus was indeed God, different from the rest of us. The line of reasoning became: if no empty tomb and physical appearances, then no resurrection. Paul believed that if there were no resurrection of Jesus then Christianity is founded on a lie. The later movement shifted a step further and influenced belief in "facts" about which Paul seemed to have either no knowledge or no interest.

Christians' belief in the resurrection of Jesus should not be dependent on a literal acceptance of the empty tomb and physical appearances stories. The *how* of Jesus' resurrection, like our own, is a mystery we have to live with. No matter how much we raise the issue for examination and debate, we will constantly and inevitably come to the conclusion that we do not know what the dynamics of entrance into eternal life are.

However, what many adult Christians recognize today is this: any notion of an actual human body leaving this planet and going somewhere else clearly belongs to myth or to fantasy. The notion cannot be taken literally. The story of Jesus' resurrection should not be intrinsically connected with it and there is no need to keep the connection.

In the face of questions being asked by adult Christians about such important issues as the resurrection, we can see how utterly inadequate is the response from some church leaders. They insist that adult education is about providing clear answers and should avoid "confusing" or "disturbing" the "simple faithful." This head-in-the-sand approach by some members of the Roman Catholic hierarchy is supported by their claim to be guardians of a "deposit of faith." They mistake adult faith education to be the task of giving adults answers contained in the "deposit," unwilling to concede that many adults are questioning the framework in which the deposit was grounded. Their message to adults and adult faith educators is, "You have a catechism with the correct answers. Make sure your thinking is in accord with what it says."

As we come, now, to the central question this book raises, let us keep in mind that what is at issue here is not only the question itself, whether Jesus is "truly God" as well as "truly man." The broader issue is adult faith education and the need for adults to speak more about what they believe and why.

Discussion Points

1. Do you believe no one had access to eternal life with God before Jesus was raised from the dead? If so, why?
2. Why is the resurrection of Jesus important to Christian faith?
3. Is the physicality of Jesus' resurrection an important issue for you?
4. What does resurrection tell you about God?

– *Chapter 7* –

Is Jesus God?

MY PREVIOUS BOOK, *Tomorrow's Catholic: Understanding God and Jesus in a New Millennium*, attempted to put into simple language present-day criticisms of the worldview in which traditional faith has been packaged. It also attempted to show how the message of Jesus has universal appeal for people who know they live in a continually expanding universe with billions and billions of galaxies. In March 1998, the Catholic archbishop of Melbourne banned the book from sale in the archdiocese, announcing it contained "serious doctrinal errors," and forbade me to speak in public on the topics of incarnation, redemption, and the Trinity. The archbishop presented me with a ten-page document outlining my "serious doctrinal errors." The document relied heavily on quotations from the *Catechism of the Catholic Church* and contained the accusation that I had "crudely misrepresented Catholic teaching." My efforts to reflect the popular belief that God somehow changed in attitude and practice toward us because of the death of Jesus was labeled "parody," despite my use of quotes from the *Catechism of the Catholic Church* to demonstrate the thinking is there also.

Shortly after this, as a test of my orthodoxy, another bishop asked me whether I believed that "Jesus was God in a way we are not." The underlying objective was to determine whether I would publicly teach that Jesus was, in classical terms, the incarnation of the Second Person of the Trinity. I had made it clear in *Tomorrow's Catholic* that I have difficulty with the worldview that necessitated this belief. The bishop had stated in his letter that faith is not linked to or dependent on a particular worldview. But it is quite clear the questions that emerged about Jesus and his role in the world were linked to the worldview and religious imagination of the time, especially the concern of access to heaven. I wanted people to explore what I consider to be an intrinsic link between worldview and belief. The issue is: if the Christian church wants to keep on teaching that Jesus is "true God and true man" and in this sense "God in a way we are not," then let the church demonstrate this without reference to a worldview which relies on dualistic thinking and a literal understanding of the Genesis story of creation and Adam's "fall." Let church leadership take contemporary people through whatever data it has, step by step, to convince them. Many people today will not be convinced if church leadership continues to resort to early Christian sources whose understanding and reasoning were linked to a worldview not considered relevant to contemporary understanding and reasoning. Whenever church leadership slips into dualistic thinking and images, whenever it slips into quoting those parts of Scripture or early Christian writings which in turn were influenced by dualistic thinking or literal understanding of Adam's "fall," let us point this out and insist on explanations free of such irrelevant concepts. All we are asking is that the church articulate its beliefs in a contemporary framework and in ways that help adults moving from a conventional stage of faith to deeper faith. It is no help to them, or the church in general, to ignore the challenge and have authority insist on unquestioning acceptance of doctrine.

Another question the bishop asked was whether I believed that only through the life and death of Jesus does humankind have access to eternal life with God. My reply stated that for most of my life I had believed so, but do so no longer because I do not believe in a God who cut us off or removed presence or friendship from us. I expressed my belief that Jesus never believed in such a God either. I could not imagine creation not being in total union with God or humankind not being in "everlasting union." The human lack of awareness of that connectedness is the problem, not the absence of connectedness.

Questions and answers concerning our connectedness with God will inevitably be different depending on whether we immerse ourselves in the mentality and imagination of early Christians or whether we immerse ourselves in the mentality and imagination more appropriate for the twenty-first century. However, some questions will not change: Who is Jesus? What was he trying to achieve? How does he answer our longings and hopes? Did Jesus make possible something that was not possible before him or did he reveal what always was, is, and will be?

Why should Christian leadership be so disturbed that people today will answer those questions differently from people in the fourth, fifth, or any previous century? After all, the intent is not to weaken or subvert Christianity. On the contrary, the intent is to make Christian faith more relevant. Faith based on yesterday's cosmology is not likely to captivate the young or the old.

One reason for the disturbance may well be that credal statements and doctrinal formulations are considered by many Christians in positions of authority to be articles of *fact* rather than articles of *faith*. This is evident also in many people still at a conventional faith stage. It is a significant factor for those clergy and members of the hierarchy who are zealous about teaching "true" or correct faith. They seem to regard faith as essentially intellectual assent to doctrinal statements that were shaped at a particular time in history to answer the questions of that time. There is a tendency to equate doctrinal statement with indisputable fact.

A recent, clear example of this occurred in November 1998 when some members of the Australian Catholic hierarchy met with senior Vatican officials, archbishops, and cardinals in charge of key sections of church governance. The meeting released its *Statement of Conclusions*. Paragraph 44, dealing with "The Sense of Sin," contains these two sentences:

> Catholics should come to understand more deeply Jesus' death as a redeeming sacrifice and an act of perfect worship of the Father effecting the remission of sins. A failure to appreciate this supreme grace would undermine the whole of Christian life.

There is little room here for people moving beyond the stage of conventional faith to ask awkward questions concerning religious imagination and worldview. It is little wonder the Roman Catholic Church is reluctant to engage the questions being raised in this book if the "whole of Christian life" is dependent on Jesus' death being a "redeeming sacrifice ... effecting the remission of sins."

It seems that somewhere within Christian tradition a very significant shift has occurred: some concepts that began as explanations of faith, born of human minds wrestling with issues in the context of the prevailing religious worldview, somehow came to be understood and taught as facts beyond questioning. Explaining, making sense of Jesus' role in human affairs in the worldview of the early Christian centuries is one thing. But holding on to that worldview and elevating explanations dependent on it into statements of fact is something else.

The *Catechism of the Catholic Church* makes a significant claim: "Faith is *certain*. It is more certain than all human knowledge, because it is founded on the very word of God who cannot lie" (no. 157; italics in original text).

It is clear that a statement such as, "The death of Jesus effected the remission of sins" is a statement of faith. Is it *certain?* Like other statements of faith it cannot be proved by empirical evidence, no matter how much any person believes it to be true. Facts are facts. Facts are demonstrable realities. You can verify them with concrete evidence. Jesus lived and died. That is a fact. But consider these two statements from the *Catechism of the Catholic Church.* Are they *certain?* Are they statements of fact or are they faith explanations dependent on a particular religious imagination?

> Christ's death . . . restores man to communion with God. (no. 613)

> . . . for the Father handed his Son over to sinners in order to reconcile us with himself. (no. 614)

We are not dealing with statements of fact or certainty here. The relevant facts connected with such statements have more to do with why people came to make these statements of faith rather than the statements themselves. We can deal with those facts. We can ask what the prevailing worldview was, or still is; we can read and see to what extent the worldview shaped or still shapes thinking. We can ask if we share the same worldview today. This is the arena of fact. There is evidence here to consider. However, church authorities insist that this evidence, the data on which reasoning depended, can in no way change the doctrinal statement even if the doctrinal statement is reliant on this data. Instead, faith statements are elevated to the level of factual statements of certainty and are then considered to be beyond questioning.

The practice of turning explanations of faith into statements of fact and hence not open to questioning is a very important issue in Christianity today. Many Christians are turning away from interpreting the life and message of Jesus in the framework of the traditional understanding of a "fall" at the beginning of human history. The images and ideas of that framework, no matter how enshrined in the *Catechism,* are simply irrelevant to their understanding of the universe, this planet, and the development of life. But when they try to articulate their Christian faith in a contemporary framework they come up against official suspicion and an insistence they must not question doctrinal conclusions shaped centuries ago. These conclusions are fact, set in concrete, incapable of being changed.

In my case, the Catholic archbishop of Melbourne demanded that I rewrite *Tomorrow's Catholic* in accord with thinking acceptable to the archbishop since it was his responsibility to ensure I was being faithful to orthodox Catholic teaching. The archbishop stressed I was expected to believe and make clear in a reediting of my book that official church teaching on the Trinity refers to an actual reality.

Here is a clear example of a faith explanation being used as a statement of fact.

Church teaching on the Trinity is rightly recognized as an inspired attempt by human minds to explain the reality of God in the context of the religious perspective of the time. But to insist that this provides incontrovertible evidence that God is actually a Trinity of Persons is a huge shift and a rather audacious claim. It is also contrary to a basic Christian theological principle that any human language and images concerning God can at best only point toward an understanding. They can never be taken as actual description.

Christian faith and understanding of God as a Trinity of Persons grew out of early Christianity's interpretation of Jesus' work of salvation. We recognize, however, that the worldview on which this was based no longer rings true to us today. The challenge for officialdom and theologians today is how to persuade people to believe that God is a Trinity when the contemporary worldview is so different from that which shaped the doctrinal definition.

If we disengage our understanding of Jesus from a dualistic worldview and a literal understanding of the Adam and Eve story, what happens to our understanding of God as a Trinity of Persons? If we think little or nothing happens, let us engage the issue and start talking about it, since there is nothing to lose and everything to gain by separating our faith from that dualism. If, on the other hand, something significant happens, let us engage the issue because intellectual integrity and genuine faith would demand we articulate what changes may flow from it.

Let us be clear. The issue here is *not* theological, spiritual, or devotional attempts to show how Trinitarian thinking can enrich the Christian understanding of sharing in God's life. There may be wonderful benefits in thinking about and relating with God as a Trinity of Persons. The issue here is Christian authority standing on a claim that its language and imagery about a Trinitarian God is factual, that this is actually who and what God is, and that Jesus of Nazareth is actually the incarnation of the Second Person of the Trinity.

Christianity is at a crossroads here. What seemed valid reasons for elevating some particular faith concepts into statements of fact in an earlier age are no longer valid reasons today. Christianity must take up the challenge to articulate its doctrinal beliefs with reasons that make sense today. Faith must build on reason. That has always been a strong principle of Christian theology. It is no help whatever to the modern mind to insist on belief solely because it is the tradition of the church. It is no help either to quote a catechism as if that now ends all discussion. The modern mind asks for reasons to believe and demands to be taken through a process that will command respect and encourage assent. This is adult faith at work.

To the question, "Do you believe Jesus is the incarnation of the pre-existent Eternal Word, the Second Person of the Blessed Trinity?" the response from many adult Christians is likely to be: "Why should I keep on believing this if I no longer give credence to the worldview which gave rise to its formulation?" This response will shock people entrenched in traditional faith language and thought patterns. It is inconceivable to them that an adult Christian could deliberately question a dogma of Christian faith. So let us be very clear about the following:

1. The onus is on those who insist on the truth of a doctrinal proposition to show in a *contemporary* worldview, devoid of allusions to dualism and scriptural literalism, why Christians should keep on believing this as an article of faith.

2. The fact that some Christians raise doubts and questions about a proposition that has long been considered essential to Christian faith ought not imply that they are "losing the faith" or are in bad faith. Their expressions of disbelief accompany a normal progression in adult faith development. They are looking to have their faith based on solid reasoning and contemporary knowledge. They are searching to make their faith personally appropriated rather than reliant on blind acceptance of authoritative teaching. Church leadership needs to be able to accompany Christians in this stage of faith development rather than restricting them.

It is a fact that many Christians have let go of various aspects of faith to which they once held. They do so and remain Christian. Some Christians find that angels, purgatory, limbo, indulgences, novenas, prayers to saints, visits to churches, and so on play little or no part in their Christian faith. It is obviously a big jump from these issues to whether one believes Jesus is the incarnation of the Second Person of the Blessed Trinity. However, many Christians are discovering a greater richness in their religion as they engage new knowledge, new insights, and new ways of understanding how God is revealed to us. They are also discovering that Jesus does not have to be radically different from the rest of humanity for the heart of his message and the insights of Pentecost to transform and give deeper meaning to life.

That brings us to the heart of the matter. What does and what does not change if we shift from believing that Jesus is "God in a way we are not"?

God still remains utterly transcendent and yet utterly immanent. God remains, even more so, the greatest Mystery of all, beyond our concepts and beyond our mistaken efforts to shape God into our notion of "person" and beyond the popular image of a male deity. God still remains Creator, Sustainer, Spirit of Surprises, Love, Life, Truth, Goodness, Source of all that exists.

God remains present to all of creation, and we will continue to believe that all of creation in some way expresses that presence. We will believe, perhaps more so, that God comes to wonderful visibility in human beings.

A significant difference is that we will no longer rely on the Genesis story of creation to tell our basic, underlying, foundational story of humankind's relationship with God. We will tell another story that has the capacity to inspire greater awe, wonder, and gratitude. We will tell a story of God working in and through what God has to work with. It will be a story with the capacity to enthrall and delight as we trace the journey of atoms in our bodies back to their presence in stars exploding billions of years ago. It will be a story on a grand scale, a story that all people on this planet can appreciate and identify with. We will want our respective Christian churches to embrace this story and to tell the story of Jesus within the framework of this story.

We will continue to make Jesus of Nazareth central to our lives and to the meaning we give to our lives. We will continue to gather around his story, because of all the stories we have, this one enlightens us and sets us free. This story sets us free from images and ideas and religious practices that bind us into fear, guilt, a sense of distance from God, a sense of our unworthiness, and religious dependence on others to bring the sacred to us. This story, if we tell it well, will enlighten us about Love in our midst and the wonder of living *in* this Love and defining the purpose of life in this faith understanding. This is a story that will affirm us and at the same time challenge us to live with great generosity, care, and compassion because in so doing we will make the reign of God evident among us.

Jesus will still be for us who are Christian the one who uniquely reveals what God is like. We will continue to believe and to proclaim that this human person incarnated God as best a human person could do so, but we will not give him a "divine nature" which the rest of us do not possess. We will question the thinking and the worldview that made that step seem necessary. We will, however, joyfully call him "divine" and our rejoicing will reflect our belief that the very same Spirit of divine Love that moved in him moves in all of us.

At the same time that we rejoice in the "saving" role of Jesus in our lives, we will appreciate that God is not more interested in or present to Christians than any other religious group. We will have a greater appreciation of God working in and through all cultures, always. This appreciation will prompt us to greater respect for the spiritual wisdom of other religious traditions. It will help us to see more clearly and

name God's present and ongoing revelation instead of being
fixated, as we have been, on protecting, preserving, and insisting upon a fourth- or fifth-century articulation of Christian
faith and what "salvation" means.

We will keep on reading our Scriptures. However, we will
read them with the understanding that they reflect and are
inspired by the Spirit of God working in and through the
cultural understandings of the time. We will be more attuned
to seeking in the Scriptures what is universally applicable. We
will read them with minds attuned to God's Spirit manifesting
itself everywhere, not confined to one religious group and not
dependent on Jesus of Nazareth for its active presence.

Many Christians could accept all of this and live Christian
life to its fullest. Their lives would be still inspired and motivated by the life and teaching of Jesus. In other words, to
shift from an understanding that Jesus is God in a way we are
not does not necessarily subvert or diminish Christian life. In
terms of personal *spirituality,* Christian living could be greatly
strengthened. Jesus does not have to be God in a way that we
are not to continue inspiring men and women to establish the
Kingdom of God in our midst.

We Christians have been accustomed to think Christianity
stands or falls on whether Jesus is "true God and true man,"
a human being with a divine "nature" that other human beings do not possess. Yet this is not the most fundamental issue
at all. The most fundamental issue is what this man's teaching and practice revealed to people of his time, and now to
our time, about the nature and presence of God and how we
connect with God. He took a clear stance on basic religious
attitudes and asked whether people would stand with him or
against him, whether they would "convert" and "be saved"
by knowing a loving God present in human love, or stay in
fear of and a sense of distance from God.

It is only when we have immersed ourselves in this fundamental issue of Jesus revealing our connectedness with God that we should raise the question whether Jesus is God in a way we are not. We can then frame the question: "Does Jesus *need to be* a unique incarnation of God in order to 'save' us?" As we have seen, early Christian thinkers, Christian tradition, and the writers of the *Catechism of the Catholic Church* thought Jesus had to be God because of the religious worldview in which they shaped their responses.

Today, however, our understanding of Jesus within the framework of the New Story encourages a different response. With Jesus still clearly and firmly at the heart of our faith vision and our spirituality, we can believe that he does not have to be God for our faith to have meaning and validity.

This change in Christian perception is quite widespread and there is not much point trying to suppress it or deny it. Rather, let us bring the issue out in the open and have public comment and discussion. The only losers in any open discussion will be people who blindly or authoritatively quote official doctrine demanding that this end all discussion. Of course many people will be disturbed, but we should not use that as an excuse for avoiding the issue. Jesus disturbed people. He would have been well aware that the process of conversion often begins with the disturbance of long-held images and ideas.

We need to be clear that the initial discussion should not be about doctrine concerning how and why Jesus is "true God." Rather, it should focus on the teaching and witness of Jesus and what he reveals to us about God and our connectedness with God. This should be done within the context of twenty-first-century knowledge about the universe and about life on this planet. This is vitally important because so often Christians enter discussion about Jesus with their minds already set on Jesus "being God." No, discuss his teaching and witness first, and *then* ask: from what we have articulated about his teaching and in the light of contemporary understanding of the cosmos, are there factors that lead us to conclude that Jesus is "true God"? If there are, let these be shared and let these be contemporary means of persuading people to accept this conclusion. This would surely be of immense value to Christianity in its need to find contemporary images and language for its preaching about Jesus. On the other hand, if the factors leading to the conclusion that Jesus is "true God" are not apparent, let us examine the consequences with honesty and courage.

On the level of personal spirituality and the adult articulation of our Christian faith, this discussion would be invaluable. For the institutional church, too, it would be invaluable. However, institutional resistance to such discussion is likely to be very strong. Any conclusions that might weaken the case for Jesus being "true God" would confront the official church with a major challenge to its authority. The traditional basis for its power and authority would be under threat. Traditional Christianity claims to be directly founded by the Son of God. It claims uniqueness among all religions because of this claim. Its authority and teaching mandate rests very much on the theological understanding that it acts as the voice of God in the world. The Roman Catholic Church is not alone in this claim. Even in quite unstructured Christian religious groups some authority figures claim to speak with God-given, not-to-be-questioned authority.

If we take the Roman Catholic Church as our example, we can readily see enormous consequences. No longer could this church make exclusive claims about being the One, True Religion. No longer could it claim that entrance into the church makes a person a member of "God's family." No longer could it claim that it is God's will that all people should be gathered into the Roman Catholic Church before the end of human history:

To reunite all his children, scattered and led astray by sin, the Father willed to call the whole of humanity together into his Son's Church. The Church is the place where humanity must rediscover its unity and salvation. (*Catechism of the Catholic Church,* no. 845)

No longer could its leaders speak as the voice of God on issues such as mandatory celibacy for clergy, the ordination of women to priestly ministry, and a whole range of other issues.

For two thousand years Christianity has built its identity on Jesus being "true God and true man." Of all issues the Christian religion will face in the new millennium, this is perhaps the most central.

Will Christianity be prepared to move beyond the limited cultural stories and limited religious worldview which shaped its identity, its purpose for existing, and its power structures? Will Christianity engage the New Story, which is far more universal and has within it the possibility of humankind embracing the reality of One Creator Spirit (with many different names and understandings) in whom we all live and move and have our being? Will Christianity work alongside all of humankind to search for and articulate a common bonding in this one Spirit?

Christianity claims to be the only religion actually founded directly by God. The claim may make sense within the narrow framework in which Christianity has traditionally interpreted the "saving" activity of Jesus, that is, within a literal understanding of one culture's creation story. But globally, that literal understanding either makes no sense to many cultures or is being abandoned by people who once believed it. Furthermore, the claim has put severe limits on Jesus' understanding of God's reign on earth. It has become too easy to identify, wrongly, the Christian religion as the only valid, visible sign of the "kingdom" or "reign" of God on earth.

At their 1998 Synod, the Roman Catholic bishops of Asia were open and forthright about the challenge to make Jesus central in the lives of Asian people while at the same time respecting the dignity and truth of the other great religions in Asia. The bishops put forward these considerations for effective preaching on Jesus to take root:

- A less theological, more human presentation of Jesus is needed. Preaching about Jesus should be set free from a theological framework which is not relevant to Asian thinking about life and the transcendent.

- The human traits of Jesus should be emphasized.

- Jesus should be presented as the one who understands the suffering of the weak.

- Jesus should be presented as the fulfillment of the yearnings of Asia expressed in the mythologies and folklore of Asian peoples.

- What the Christian message has in common with other religions should be the starting point.

- It would not be prudent to present Jesus as the only savior immediately. He should first be presented as the perfect human being.

- The uniqueness of Jesus, though theologically correct, may not be the best place to start.

- For some, the expression "Christ the only savior" is "too aggressive."

- Many Asians do not see the church as a sign of God's presence or as a teacher of spirituality. It is not seen as a praying church.*

---

* "Doing It the Asian Way," special report, *The Tablet* (May 16, 1998), 647–49.

If all branches of institutional Christianity took a lead from the bishops of Asia and stepped back from seeing themselves as the dispensers, guardians, and controllers of God's presence and action in the world, this would surely send a significant message to the world. For Christian churches this could be *the* movement of God's Spirit in these times.

However, we know that if we wait for institutions to change and adapt, our waiting may well be in vain. Herein lies the frustration and disillusionment being experienced by many Christians today. They have moved in their spirituality; they have a faith vision of life that embraces all of humankind. They think and act beyond the limitations of the church that nurtured them in faith. However, they see their church in its institutional expressions grimly holding on to past formulations, images, language, and practices. Many Christians now rely less on institutional forms of religion and more on their spirituality and their exchanges with people who share their faith journey for affirmation, growth, and challenge. We even find the question being asked whether institutional religion has a place in the future. It probably will not have a place if it refuses to embrace new thinking and understanding about the cosmos and our place in it. It will have a place if it reverts to being and doing what it ought to be and do: an organized way of ensuring that the insights of Jesus of Nazareth are relevant to the questions and longings of people at any time of history. This entails helping people in their historical times to live a dynamic Christian spirituality that engages shifts of understanding and new knowledge about themselves, their world, and how God might be acting.

Discussion Points

1. What reasoning in favor of Jesus being the incarnation of the Second Person of the Trinity seems persuasive and meaningful to you?

2. What reasoning and what factors move you to question the traditional Christian belief that Jesus is "truly God" as well as "truly man"?

3. What difference would it make to you personally and the way you live if you believed that Jesus was not "God in a way we are not"?

– Chapter 8 –

Implications for Liturgy

M ORE AND MORE committed adult Christians are saying that the images and language of formalized religion no longer sit comfortably with them. These adults are questioning and searching, moving beyond the childhood packaging of their faith. Many do courses in theology and spirituality. However, even without the benefit of such courses, many no longer accept, for example, the idea of an original "fall." They find themselves caught up in a domino effect: what about this belief or practice and what about that belief or practice? The questions will not go away. These adults find that formalized religion is increasingly failing to nourish and to support their developing understanding of faith. Going to their usual church service seems like a step back in time and in faith. They want to be encouraged and affirmed in their faith development but encounter religious services locked into outdated images and language that church authority decrees are timeless and will never change.

These adults find themselves being jolted by liturgical and credal language they had in the past spoken or heard week after week, without any questioning. For example:

God from God, Light from Light, true God from true God, begotten, not made, of one Being with the Father. Through him all things were made. For us men and our salvation he came down from heaven. (The Nicene Creed)

Lord Jesus, you are mighty God and Prince of Peace. Lord have mercy.

Many people familiar with these words suddenly find themselves questioning the words and their associated understandings. In the recent past they may never have imagined they would question whether and why they should believe that Jesus is "mighty God" who "came down from heaven." Now they find themselves exploring and questioning the religious imagination they inherited as children concerning humankind's basic relationship with God.

Is Jesus "mighty God" who came down from heaven for our salvation? This is a crucial question, isn't it? If we abandon the worldview which necessitates Jesus being "mighty God" in order for us to gain access to God's glory, then we will find ourselves questioning more and more liturgical and credal images and language.

The outdated worldview on which so much of our liturgical language is based is starkly evident once people become aware of it. The language then loses its capacity to address and contact people at their level of faith development. It leads to further questioning and often to a dissatisfaction with liturgy. Consider these examples from the Roman Catholic Eucharistic ritual:

In Christ man restores to man the gift of everlasting life. (Preface of Christmas III)

What is meant by saying Christ "restores" the gift? Why should we believe the gift was ever lost?

He has come... to lead mankind from exile into your heavenly kingdom. (Preface of Christmas II)

From where has Jesus come? Why are we using language about being in "exile" from God? Why is the focus on the "heavenly" kingdom rather than God's kingdom or reign on earth?

> He has opened the gates of heaven to receive his faithful people. His death is our ransom from death: his resurrection is our rising to life. (Preface of Easter II)

Even allowing for "gates of heaven" being symbolic language, what religious imagination is at work here concerning humankind's access to God? Why are we using "ransom" language concerning the death of Jesus?

Roman Catholic liturgy constantly proclaims that we are reconciled with God through Jesus' death:

> Calling to mind the death your Son endured for our salvation.... See the Victim whose death has reconciled us to yourself. (Eucharistic Prayer III)

> By suffering on the cross he freed us from unending death, and by rising he gave us eternal life. (Preface of Sundays in Ordinary Time II)

> As he offered his body on the cross, his perfect sacrifice fulfilled all others. As he gave himself into your hands for our salvation, he showed himself to be the priest, the altar and the lamb of sacrifice. (Preface of Easter V)

> He offered himself as a victim for our deliverance. (Preface of the Holy Eucharist I)

> As priest he offered his life on the altar of the cross and redeemed the human race by this one perfect sacrifice of peace. (Preface of Christ the King)

> He chose to die that he might free all men from dying. (Preface of Christian Death II)

He put an end to death. (Eucharistic Prayer II)

He was taken up to heaven in their sight to claim for us
a share in his divine life. (Preface of the Ascension II)

Most Christian churches could find parallels with these examples. It is hardly surprising that the images such language
conveys about God and about our relationship with God raise
questions and lead to dissatisfaction with official liturgy.

The most alarming dropout from regular church attendance in the Roman Catholic Church today is not in the
youth bracket. Young people are generally not committed to
regular attendance. We often ring alarm bells on this score,
when really we should be alarmed by the number of committed adults who have given up or are giving up on liturgies
that no longer sustain and nourish them in their faith. Not
only are they giving up on liturgy, they are also giving up
on clerics who no longer sustain and nourish them in their
faith development. Yet, in discussions about how to remedy
the situation (surely a matter of the highest priority) church
leadership will not address the fact that an "ageless" liturgy,
steeped in a theological understanding of Jesus' death "recon-
ciling us with God," no longer adequately expresses the faith
and spirituality of many adult Christians. As we have already
seen, the Roman Catholic Church at the official level remains
steadfast in the belief that "the whole of Christian life would
be undermined" by a failure to appreciate Jesus' death as a
"redeeming sacrifice...effecting the remission of sins."

Church authorities seem prepared to let these adults go
rather than acknowledge there is a major shift going on
throughout Christianity. These adult Christians will continue
to be Christian, will seek support for their faith journey, but
more and more will give up on their local church community. They will find a nourishing experience of church in small
groups. The next stage will inevitably be that an increasing

number of these small groups will enact their own style of eucharistic rituals—without an ordained minister—and will find it meaningful and supportive. They will reflect on the Scriptures and share experiences and prayer. They will eat and drink together, mindful of the Spirit being with them as the Spirit was with Jesus. They will pledge themselves to be the Body of Christ for others and will pledge to support one another in the challenges of living in the Spirit of Jesus. They will be very conscious of themselves as "church."

This situation might never have arisen if authority figures in the institutional church had used their power and influence to ensure that the church stayed tuned to contemporary expressions of Christian spirituality. Vatican II caught the mood and direction in the Roman Catholic Church. Liturgical change followed rapidly and dramatically. In recent times, however, a reactionary movement has strengthened. A watchdog mentality is very much alive in the Vatican and throughout the Roman Catholic Church. Authority is fearful that things have got out of hand and that a return to tight, rigid control is now necessary. In this climate liturgy remains subservient to and expressive of "correct" theological thinking. No changes to liturgical language or practice that could give witness to different ways of perceiving God's activity in our world will be considered or tolerated.

However, liturgy is meant to be the action of the people who make up the "Body" of Christ; it is meant to be expressive of their Christian faith vision of life. If the theology underpinning contemporary spirituality has shifted from the theology underpinning the traditional liturgy, then adjustments have to be made to liturgy. Does liturgy exist primarily to protect and preserve a given theological framework or does it exist primarily to reflect the "story" people want to tell about their relationship with God and how Jesus fits into that story? Should liturgy be tightly controlled or should there be a flexibility allowing for "the Body" to have some determination of its form?

The challenge is to rescue liturgy from a theological perspective that is no longer relevant to people's lives. Church authority will rightly want to exercise control over official liturgy, but in doing so it must accept and be influenced by the fact that adults will continue to abandon the church's official worship in large numbers if significant adaptations are not made to its language and imagery.

Christian liturgy could be rescued from an outdated theological perspective.

It could celebrate the life and teaching of Jesus who reveals to us the wonder of God's presence in all people. It could celebrate and proclaim the Old Testament Scriptures, especially the prophetic call to people who believed they lived in covenant with God to build a just and compassionate society. It could articulate and celebrate how the sacred is present in all aspects of human life, even in brokenness, pain, tragedy, and darkness. It could summon us and call us to be more aware of the presence of our God all around us. It could challenge us to look the way Jesus looked, hear the way Jesus heard, touch one another's lives the way Jesus touched lives with respect and compassion. It could constantly affirm us in the conviction that we are the "Body" in whom the Spirit moves and acts. It could be the bearer of the good news that God's reign is present in all decent human endeavors. It could and should use language, images, and patterns of thought that are relevant to the people in attendance, so that the liturgy in Asia might be quite different from the liturgy in Italy, North America, or Africa.

We would find a different emphasis in the way the major liturgical feasts, Christmas, Easter, and Pentecost, are celebrated.

At Christmas we would shift from the traditional focus on

a virgin birth and a literal acceptance of the infancy stories. The shift would be accompanied by access to Scripture scholarship, which could help us appreciate the infancy stories even better if we avoid a literal reading of the texts. Liturgy would help us engage the same question the writers of those stories engaged: who is this child for us? We, however, will shape our response in the light of the New Story. We will celebrate that this baby, human like the rest of us, will grow, mature, ask searching questions, shape convictions, take enormous risks, and give himself completely to the service of God's Spirit.

Who is this child for us? We believe we see the best possible revelation of God in the man this child became. We believe his insights and teaching about God are good news that sets us free and helps us articulate direction and meaning for human existence.

We will tell this story, though, with the conviction that God's Spirit is active everywhere and that God's revelation is not confined to this person, this place, this event, and this time in history.

Christmas will touch us deeply because there is an innocence here, as there is with every baby born into this world. There is parental hope and dreams. There is the wonder of God at work in our midst. There is appreciation for the way this child will reveal God's active and loving presence. There is hope here for all of us to share.

Christmas will touch us because it is a story challenging us to turn upside down where we look for the sacred. This story tells us that the sacred is in the mess of a stable, in events that can go horribly wrong, in the lowliest of people like shepherds, in people of different cultures—like magi—in the love between a man and a woman and their baby. We will proclaim and celebrate God-with-us.

Holy Week will not be the story of a god-figure dying and being raised as a victim for our deliverance. It will be the story of a man, human like us, who gave everything for the sake of God's reign and who died in failure. It will be the story of a man who had a wonderful understanding of human existence and felt the power of God's Spirit working in and through him as he shared his understanding. But his dream was shattered and the last days of his life saw his faith severely tested by abandonment, rejection, failure, cruelty, and a shameful death. This man had to reach into the depths of his being when life would have tempted him to despair. He would have experienced the ache of faith that touches most of our lives: How can we believe God is good and loving when this happens to us? Where is God in all of this? Can I believe there is another way of living on in God beyond this darkness and beyond my inevitable death?

Good Friday will focus on faith rather than "ransom" or "victim." Good Friday will resonate with our own struggles and pain, our hope and our faith. It will be the story of the triumph of the human spirit, a story we are all familiar with, not just in the life of Jesus but also in the stories of all the fathers, mothers, husbands, wives, children, brothers, sisters, and friends who have died. We will recognize and be grateful for the fact that it was the manner of Jesus' death and his faith in God's fidelity that gave and still gives courage, hope, and faith to our relatives, our friends, and us.

Easter Sunday will flow with joy from Good Friday. It will not be the "first time" story of God raising someone to life or the story of the gates of heaven now being opened by God in response to Jesus' death. It will be a celebration that the life and death of Jesus revealed the constancy of God's loving presence. It will focus on the good news that because of Jesus we can articulate our belief that living in love has an eternal connectedness with living on in God after death. It will celebrate a Christian optimism about all of creation, that beyond death and destruction there is the reality of new life.

It will deepen belief that access to eternal life with God is not dependent on being a Christian or dependent on professing any particular religious creed—we share access with all people who live in love. It will challenge us to live and work with all people in the conviction we are all God's people.

Pentecost will not be the story of a group of people receiving a Spirit they previously did not possess. Nor will it be the story of exclusive possession of the Spirit. It will be the story of God's Spirit always actively present in creation. It will be the story of what happens when people see a man totally give his life to allowing that Spirit move in him and what can happen if they imitate him. It will be the story of people becoming aware that the same Spirit that lived and moved in Jesus lived and moved in them. It is the story of people becoming aware of what is and what could be. Pentecost is the Wow! story of human existence, of who we are and who we are called to be. Pentecost is the story to affirm that we are all temples of God's Spirit—every one of us. This is the story the church needs to tell again and again because it articulates what the purpose and mission of the church are.

We would not be praying prayers that beg God to send the Spirit upon us or to grant us a share in God's life. Our prayers would affirm that we are already richly blessed with such graciousness from God. Our liturgical gathering should affirm us and motivate us to share this understanding of human existence. And when we do so, we are "church," spreading the good news.

In the Roman Catholic community we would be more focused on the "body" of Christ being the people rather than being focused on the "body" being a sacred object. We would be less focussed on disputes concerning "real" presence and how that works and who has it and who does not have it. We would appreciate that Christianity would benefit greatly by shared communion in which we are aware of our shared com-

mitment to "be" the body of Christ in all we do. Our shared
commitment to giving expression to God's reign among us
is far more important than doctrinal issucs that divide us.
The language, images, and ideas in our "eucharistic prayers"
would need to change significantly. Can this be done and still
be faithful to the story of Jesus and still resonate with a pattern of prayer to which we are accustomed? Yes, undoubtedly.
For example:

> We give you thanks
> Creator Spirit beyond all imagining,
> for the wonderful gift of reflective awareness
> that allows us to recognize and name your presence in
>   our universe.
> Everything we have; everything we see; everything we
>   do;
> everyone we love and everyone who loves us
> reveals your sustaining presence
> and our total dependence on your presence.
>
> We marvel and wonder at the size and complexity of
>   our universe.
> We marvel and wonder at the development of life on
>   this planet.
> We thank you that your presence "charges" this life and
>   all that exists.
> We recognize that human life gives you a particular way
>   of expressing yourself
> and that in us you can sing and dance, speak and write,
>   love and create.
>
> Conscious that we live, move, and have our being *in*
>   you,
> we give you thanks for people throughout history
> who have affirmed your loving presence in all people

and who have challenged people to give witness to your
    presence
by lives characterized by mercy, gratitude, compassion,
    generosity, and forgiveness.

We thank you for Jesus of Nazareth
who loved so greatly
and taught so clearly and courageously
that he was able to set people free
from images and ideas and religious practices
that bound them into fear and a false sense of separation
    from you.
Through him we have learned how our loving is a
    sharing in your life.
In him we see your presence challenging us to make
    your reign on earth more visible.

We remember the night before he died, when he took
    bread,
gave you thanks for everything he had,
broke the bread and shared it with his friends
asking them to remember his total surrender to you
and his enduring love for each of them.

This is my body, given for you.

Likewise, knowing his life was to be poured out,
he shared the cup of wine with them.

This is my blood shed for you. A covenant of love.

We believe that like all people who lived in love and
    died in love
Jesus died into your eternal loving embrace.
We are thankful that his story grounds our belief in our
    own eternal, loving connectedness with you

and our belief that we are in communion with all our
relatives and friends who have died.

We pray for all who allow the mind and heart and spirit
of Jesus to motivate their actions.
We pray that Christian leadership may be open and
affirming, creative and challenging.
We pray that all Christians might better recognize,
acknowledge, and acclaim your presence in all
people, at all times, in all places.

For ourselves gathered here we ask the grace
to be who and what we ritualize here: the "body of
Christ,"
people committed by our "Amen" to allowing your
Spirit to move freely in our lives.
We thank you that we have gathered here as the body
of Christ;
we rejoice in the giftedness of each person here;
we are grateful for who we are for each other.
We consider ourselves blessed *in* and *by* you.
May we be truly eucharistic in all we do.
To this prayer we give our *Amen.*

If liturgy were to move in the direction being proposed here
it would immediately engage our lived experience, affirm us,
connect us more closely with the story of Jesus, connect with
the New Story about earth and the universe and challenge us
to give witness to the Spirit moving in our lives.

The question is whether liturgy will be "allowed" to do it.

What we can be certain of is this: if official liturgy is not
allowed to shift from its present theological framework, the
number of adult Christians seeking other places to ritualize
and nurture their faith will dramatically increase. Adults moving from a conventional faith stage will be reacting not only

against the language and imagery of the official liturgy; they will be reacting also against bigness and anonymity. They will be seeking smaller groups where relating and sharing are easier and welcomed and where they feel they can no longer be manipulated into docile acceptance of what is being offered.

Discussion Points

1. How comfortably do the images and language of formalized religion sit with you?

2. What reflections would you add to how Christmas, Easter, and Pentecost could be celebrated?

– Chapter 9 –

Implications for Ministry

EVERY CHRISTIAN COMMUNITY seeks to act as Jesus acted, wanting to make the same Spirit that moved in Jesus visible in society today. Looking, hearing, touching, and speaking as Jesus did should be the characteristics of any Christian community. It follows that the heart of Christian ministry must be to recognize, name, and affirm the presence of God's Spirit in people's lives and to call people to act in accord with this presence. Affirmation and the call to give witness— these are two features of Jesus' approach to ministry. They are also key features of the Pentecost experience and lay the foundation for all Christian ministry.

Jesus' ministry flowed from his belief that living in love was living in God. Much of his ministry consisted in trying to persuade people to share his belief and to allow that belief to transform their actions.

If Christian ministry seriously modeled itself on Jesus' practice of ministry it would bring changes to the way ministry operates in many Christian communities today. A prerequisite for any person ministering on behalf of the Christian community should be the ability to be with people in their experiences of being vulnerable, broken, joyful, needy, searching, and questioning. Being *with* people. Jesus exemplified this skill. People recognized his compassion, his ability to understand their situation, to identify with them.

Being with people in the way Jesus related with people would avoid a common pitfall of Christian ministry: the minister thinking he or she brings the sacred to people. The thinking is not uncommon, for example, among ministers taking communion to the sick. Nor is it uncommon in preaching, sacramental practice, and pastoral visitation. It is evident when a minister assumes an official role and people being ministered to experience the role rather than the person. It is evident when the minister is more intent on properly dispensing something sacred, whether it be by word or action, than on being *with* the person.

Without empathy ministry loses its human face and is unable to be present to the lived situation. Without empathy, ministry becomes a Band-Aid, a pat on the head, a magic formula or pious platitudes. Without empathy, preaching, worship, and Christian ministry will avoid touching on the important life issues such as loneliness, pain, disappointment, doubts, questioning, fears, limitations, sickness, death, aging, change of life, depression, disillusionment, parenting, loss, grief, sexuality, feeling worthwhile, feeling powerless, knowing the power and joy of love—and a multitude of other issues and concerns that affect our lives. These experiences, by the very fact they are common to all believers and ministers alike, have the capacity to move people to deeper levels of awareness and questioning. They have the capacity to bond Christian ministry with the lives of people through the search for understanding and through shared compassion. These experiences can be the means to help people articulate more clearly and meaningfully the reality of God's Spirit at work in their lives. This is the arena for creative ministry, a ministry capable of naming the sacred in people's lives, of affirming the presence of the sacred and of calling people to live in the confidence of that sacred presence with them.

Affirmation is important in both ministry and liturgy. We

need to be affirmed again and again in the belief that our God is intimately a part of the ups and downs of our everyday lives. We live in love; we live in God. We are earthen vessels; we are temples of God's Spirit. We are ordinary bread; we are Body. We are blessed; we are broken; we are given. And we believe that in these lived experiences there is a sacred presence sustaining and giving meaning to our lives.

This sustaining, sacred presence is the basis of the Christian belief that there is more to life than meets the eye. The belief that everything is charged with God's presence is the heart of our faith, just as it was the heart of Jesus' preaching.

Early Christian thought and practice turned to "sacraments" to help people encounter the unseen presence of God, to celebrate God's graciousness, and to pledge themselves to live in accord with God's gracious presence with them. Baptism was the public commitment to live in love and thus to live in God. It was a pledge to the community: I will turn from sin; I will allow the Spirit that moved in Jesus to move in my life; I promise that you will see in my life the mind and heart and actions of Jesus. Gathering for Eucharist was not only to celebrate the memory of Jesus; it was also to ritualize that the people present were "the Body" of Christ. They pledged themselves to *be* that Body in the way they lived. They believed in the reality of God's Spirit in them, and they pledged themselves to give witness to that Spirit.

Unfortunately, Christian thought and practice in the Middle Ages adopted an approach to sacraments that reduced them to liturgical rituals that brought the sacred to people. This understanding strengthened the dependency model of church. Most Christians considered themselves to be distant from God, were fearful of judgment and hell, and were dependent on a middle-management group, priests, to bring the sacred to them through the sacraments. Sacramental theology and disputes at the time centered on how the sacramental ritual worked and what it conferred on the recipient. This effectively turned sacramental understanding on its head. Sacraments no longer highlighted the abiding, consistent, sustaining presence of God in people's lives. Rather, sacraments became a means of

- taking away original sin, ensuring entrance into heaven, and gaining entrance into the church (Baptism);
- bringing "Jesus" to people at communion (Eucharist);
- ensuring God's forgiveness (Penance);
- granting graces to strengthen the marriage bond (Marriage);
- conferring the gifts of the Holy Spirit and making people "adult" members in the church or "soldiers of Christ" (Confirmation);
- conferring powers that the rest of the body of Christ did not have (Priesthood);
- and bringing God's healing power (Anointing of the Sick).

The Reformation split Christianity on several issues. The nature and number of sacraments was one of them. Today the important issue for Christianity concerning the sacraments is not so much their number, but how to recover and develop a well-grounded Christian sacramental understanding and how best to use the sacraments we have. In particular, can our Christian sacramental consciousness and practice have application and meaning to committed Christians on the one hand, and, on the other hand, have relevance and meaning for Christians who do not commit themselves to institutional belief and practice? Roman Catholic parish communities are faced with both situations on a weekly basis with requests for baptisms, marriages, and funerals from people who may be closely associated, loosely associated, or not associated in any way with the parish community.

How is the church community to respond to "nonpractic-ing" people who knock on the door seeking baptism for their child or a church wedding for themselves or a funeral service for a relative? What sort of service can be provided when the prescribed language, gestures, and symbols of the ritu-als are only remotely relevant or meaningful to them, if at all? Adhering faithfully to the structure and formal language of the baptismal, wedding, or funeral ritual can often create unease and awkwardness and lead to a sense of not being welcome.

Generally, these "nonpracticing" people are perceived to be problematic, since they are considered not to belong to the worshiping community. However, rather than being a problem to deal with, these people and these instances are a challenge to Christian communities and Christian ministry. It sounds too simplistic to ask, "What would Jesus do in such circumstances?" yet the teaching and practice of Jesus do pro-vide guidelines that are relevant and can be applied to a wide range of situations.

Jesus' preaching concerning the reign of God was inclusive and universal in its scope. All human beings in and through their loving and being neighbor to one another make God's reign effective and visible. This is neither culturally nor geo-graphically limited. It does not depend on what we believe about Jesus; it does not rest on intellectual assent to any "defined" doctrines. Live in love, and you make God's pres-ence and reign visible. This fundamental teaching of Jesus has nothing to do with belonging to a particular religion. Nor does the reality it points to—that living in love is living in God—cease if people withdraw from formalized religion.

What formalized religion does, if it works properly, is help people name, articulate, own, and ritualize this reality. For-malized religion does not make it happen. It is neither the guardian of God's presence nor its dispenser. No, the reality is out there in people's lives and God's reign is being made visible in all sorts of ways.

Based on the teaching and example of Jesus, the following guidelines are important for Christian communities ministering to people in these times of great change:

- Constantly affirm the presence of the sacred in people's lives. Name it, give examples, preach about it, and do all this in simple, everyday language.

- Act and speak not as dispensers or guardians of the sacred, but as proclaimers that human loving and decency are intimately connected with the sacred.

- Be gracious, welcoming, and generous with the "lost," the "crowd," the people outside the laws of religion and people who have lost faith in religion.

- Take risks; be prepared to be "unorthodox" if compassion and pastoral effectiveness call for it. Jesus did this to great effect.

- Seek what is common ground, not in terms of a religious package of beliefs that must be accepted, but in terms of our human experience of the Mystery we call "God." If doctrine needs explaining, articulate its importance for and relevance to lived experience.

- Look outward, beyond one's own religious community and concerns. Look especially to the concerns of social justice and ecumenism.

- Act against evil. Do not tolerate behavior that is clearly contrary to the Spirit of love.

- Give people due authority and power by trusting that the Spirit of God works in the "body" of the faithful and needs to be heard.

These guidelines have the potential to nourish vibrant Christian communities whose members are inspired and motivated by the message of Jesus to make God's reign visible in a world that desperately needs the "light of Christ." They also have the capacity to make "nonpracticing" Christians feel welcomed and to help them encounter a church that is meaningful and supportive.

Let us take, for example, John and Mary, who are seeking marriage in the church. They believe in God and were once baptized, but have had no contact with any church community and have no intention of initiating ongoing contact. What should be the starting point here?

Like Jesus, we surely should start with a belief that the Spirit of God is present in this couple's lives, even if they would not name their love for each other as "living in God." We are face to face with the reign of God being played out in the lives of these two people despite their lack of awareness of it. This lack of awareness is precisely what Jesus encountered among the "crowd" and what he tried to address in his preaching.

How would Jesus converse with John and Mary? How would he tap into their lived experience? How would he want them to be affected by meeting and talking with him? What convictions about love and about God would he want to share with them? Would he use formal religious language or would he use the language and images relevant to their own lives and experience?

Jesus' practice was to build on the situation he encountered. He encountered people being neighbor, visiting, caring, being generous and ready to forgive. He built on their experiences of love and concern for each other by naming this as the arena for meeting the sacred and making God's presence visible and effective among them. If we follow this practice of Jesus, there is no reason why John and Mary should not have a joyful and meaningful sacramental experience that builds on what is already present: their love for each other. The ritual would allow them to name and articulate their love for each other and to pledge themselves to give witness to their love. The ritual would also name for them and everyone present the Christian belief that they actually "live in God and that God lives in them." The ritual can express the belief that they give witness to the reign of God in the world through their loving, even if John and Mary find this difficult to believe at this stage of their lives. The commitment to love and its responsibilities, along with naming God's presence in the loving, in no way falls short of what Jesus asked of anyone in his lifetime.

Christian rituals will have to change significantly to build on particular situations. Take adult baptism for example. Baptism for someone who is publicly professing commitment to the church community ought to have its own particular focus which names and articulates this commitment, uses symbols to express commitment, and then publicly ritualizes it. All this would happen in the context of the story of Jesus, the call to discipleship and bonding with the church community.

However, in the case of parents with little or no contact with the church community presenting a child for baptism, the ritual would be different in its emphasis. It would build on the parents' commitment to love. Preparation for the ritual would focus on three key questions: Will you love this child with all your heart and soul? Do you believe your love for each other and your child is an expression of God's love? Do you see ongoing contact with this church community as desirable, significant, relevant, or helpful in your commitment to love? If after conversation and instruction the couple were not prepared to answer affirmatively to the first two questions then there would be no point in participating in the ritual. But if they are prepared to say "yes" then the ritual can express how Jesus would welcome and affirm this family. While exploration of the third question is an important part of preparation for the ritual, the significant issue is that commitment to ongoing contact with the church community need not be a prerequisite for this baptism. Rather there could be a hope that a welcoming, affirming experience of a church ritual could lead to further contact, just as Jesus might have hoped that an encounter and a conversation with him might lead people to a conversion experience.

Encountering and conversing with Jesus is a privilege that people do not have today. However, Christian ministry seeks to make that experience as real and as visible as it can through the words and actions of the minister, ordained or nonordained. Attention to the guidelines mentioned above could help all Christian ministers to give witness to the same "Spirit" that characterized the ministry of Jesus. In the Roman Catholic community the guidelines could also be useful in ministries currently curtailed by the church, especially ministry to the divorced and remarried and ministry to gays and lesbians. The guidelines are applicable also for such current issues as married clergy, the ordination of women, intercommunion with other Christian churches, and the use of the third rite of Reconciliation. While the evidence suggests that God's Spirit is moving among people creating awareness of new possibilities and new directions for ministry, church law and disciplinary measures preclude movement in new directions. The Gospels suggest that Jesus would be more daring and innovative and less fearful that people would mistake his compassion as weakness or as an erosion of his moral standards.

Discussion Points

1. Using Jesus' ministry as your focus, what other elements would you add to the guidelines on page 127?

2. Imagine you are to *preach* at a Christian funeral. The person who died lived a good life but had no contact with the church for most of his or her life. How might your preaching be shaped so that it is realistic and thoroughly Christian?

3. In what areas of official church ministry would you like to see significant changes?

– Chapter 10 –

The New Story and "catholic" Theology

I N THE ROMAN CATHOLIC CHURCH the word "Catholic" is often used in a restrictive and narrow sense. This restrictive usage reflects official expectation that "orthodox," correct thinking about God and Jesus can be found only within the traditional framework of fall-redemption theology and doctrine reliant on that framework. Religious imagination and theological speculation that operate outside the bounds of this framework are not considered "Catholic." The ideas raised in this book are likely to be judged as beyond the bounds of what is acceptable "Catholic" theology. The charge is made by some people: you are no longer a Catholic if you step beyond those defined boundaries.

The irony is that this attitude to correct "Catholic" thinking does not reflect the *Catechism of the Catholic Church's* definition of "catholic" as " 'universal' in the sense of 'according to the totality' or 'in keeping with the whole' " (no. 830).

The *Catechism* expands its definition to include the missionary task of taking the message of Jesus to the entire world. However, the basic understanding of catholic can be of help as we contemplate the issues and shifts facing Christianity today: our theologizing must be done in the context of the

132

whole or total picture. It must be done in the context of the twenty-first century's broad and ever-expanding knowledge about our universe and this planet's place in the universe. It must be done "in keeping with the whole" contemporary knowledge about the development of life on this planet and in particular what we know about the emergence of human life. It must be done with belief in the all-embracing, active presence of God's Spirit.

In this sense, all Christian theologizing should be "catholic," seeking to articulate its understanding of God and Jesus in today's bigger and broader picture of creation and life.

The Roman Catholic Church at official levels, however, will not sanction thinking and operating within a wider perspective. Church authority is more intent on judgment about whether teaching conforms to "a deposit of faith" than on expanding the horizons of theological thought. Theologians find themselves kept in check by threat of dismissal or censure if they publicly step beyond the precise and technical language of early church formulations of doctrine. For example, to state that Jesus is a "human person" is considered to be heretical by those members of the Roman Catholic hierarchy and by those Roman Catholic theologians who will not extend their thinking about Jesus beyond the doctrinal boundaries set in the fifth century.

The Second Vatican Council gave hope that the Roman Catholic Church would change from a defensive, suspicious attitude to "the world" to engagement with the signs of the times and the task of renewal in keeping with those signs. The 1966 Abbott edition of *The Documents of Vatican II* has "A Response" by Robert McAfee Brown to the "Pastoral Constitution on the Church in the Modern World." He praises the document for its "positive attitude towards the world," including "a willingness on the part of the Church to learn from the world as well as speak to the world." He quotes two assertions from Article 4: that Christians must "recognize and understand the world in which we live," and that the church has always had the duty "of scrutinizing the signs of the times and of interpreting them in the light of the gospel." He makes the interesting observation that earlier drafts of the document had expressed a "clearer" willingness to learn from the world with the statement, "We should listen to the voice of God . . . in the voice of the times." * The subtle change here is indicative of present-day Vatican engagement with the signs of the times concerning our understanding of Jesus and the nature of "salvation." Is the Vatican listening to the "voice of God . . . in the voice of the times"—like the voice of the bishops from Asia and voices telling a New Story—and responding to what the "voice of God" might be suggesting? Or is the Vatican going through the motions of listening—like calling the bishops of Asia to Rome for a Synod—but manifestly ignoring the voices because they do not fit in with the way the Vatican insists the "deposit of faith" must operate in the modern world?

This manner of engagement mirrors the approach outlined early in chapter 2 of this book, where we saw that many of us with our conventional faith firmly in place faced the world and tried to fit the rest of the world into our clearly established religious ideas and convictions.

And what many of us have discovered and continue to discover is that this approach no longer works. What we discovered was that we were not sufficiently "catholic" in our thinking and in our attitudes.

Early church history illustrates a way for a truly "catholic" theology to develop. The church community engaged the world around it, moving beyond its own familiar territory

---

*Walter Abbott, ed., *The Documents of Vatican II* (New York: America Press, 1966), 310.

because the church is essentially missionary in nature. It engaged that world and immersed itself in the questions and issues concerning the meaning of human existence and human connectedness with the Transcendent. The church community brought to this encounter the teaching of Jesus and insights gained from their belief that God had raised Jesus from death. Jesus was presented as the answer to the religious questions and longings of the time. As the "good news" was spread far and wide questions arose about who Jesus had to be in order to be the answer to some of those questions and longings. Two thousand years later the church is being challenged, as it will be in every age, to follow the same pattern. Be missionary, step out and engage the world, the world of today with its knowledge and understanding of the universe, engage the questions that arise from the New Story and from cultures vastly different from European culture. Bring the story of Jesus to the New Story and to these varying cultures and show how Jesus remains savior, light, Christ, hope, and good news for people everywhere.

But the church must listen and learn in order to do this well. It has to reverse the now disastrous policy of insisting it has nothing new to learn, that its primary task is to hand on the "truths" that it and it alone possesses.

Yes, on many levels the church engages the world of today, but in the realm of theology Roman Catholic church authority resists, condemns, isolates, and imposes bans on theologians who push across the edge of acceptable "Catholic" teaching. While professing to be "catholic" it will not engage the urgent need to reshape Christian imagination, ideas, and language "in keeping with the whole." Not only will it not engage this urgent need, it clearly continues to adopt a stance in which it sets its identity as an exclusive bearer of salvation against the rest of the world and other religious movements. Anchored in the belief that it alone has the fullness of revealed truth and that its Scriptures alone are divinely inspired, it continues to face the world not as a listener to where and how the universal presence of God's Spirit might be moving and speaking but as dispenser and guardian of what it considers to be the Spirit's exclusive gift to it of salvation.

In August 2000 the Congregation for the Doctrine of the Faith issued a "Declaration," *Dominus Iesus,* "On the Unicity and Salvific Universality of Jesus Christ and the Church." * The declaration addresses perceived errors in contemporary theology and states positions which must be "firmly believed" by theologians and the faithful. It is fascinating to see what beliefs we Roman Catholics must hold as we engage the world—and to which Roman Catholic theologians must give public assent if their teaching is to carry the blessing or approval of the Congregation:

Although "salvation" is nowhere defined—puzzling, since the word and the process can be understood in quite differing ways—it is clearly linked to the death of Jesus. Jesus is "the perfect man who has restored that likeness to God in the children of Adam which had been disfigured since the first sin.... As an innocent lamb he merited life for us by his blood which he freely shed. In him God reconciled us to himself and to one another, freeing us from the bondage of the devil and of sin" (no. 10).

With this clearly established we are to hold that "the action of the Spirit is not outside or parallel to the action of Christ. There is only one salvific economy of the One and Triune God, realized in the mystery of the incarnation, death and resurrection of the Son of God, actualized with the cooperation of the Holy Spirit, and extended in its salvific value to all humanity and to the entire universe" (no. 12).

Jesus, and Jesus "alone, as Son of God made man, crucified

---

*English texts quoted are from the Vatican web site: *www.vatican.va.*

and risen, by the mission received from the Father and in the power of the Holy Spirit, bestows revelation and divine life to all humanity and to every person" (no. 13).

The "hypothesis of the inspired value of the sacred writings of other religions" is rejected. The only sacred writings inspired by the Holy Spirit are "the canonical books of the Old and New Testaments" (no. 8).

"Above all else, it must be firmly believed that the Church, a pilgrim now on earth, is necessary for salvation: the one Christ is the mediator and the way of salvation." The church has "in God's plan, an indispensable relationship with the salvation of every human being" (no. 20).

"God has willed that the Church founded by Jesus Christ be the instrument for the salvation of humanity." "... If it is true that the followers of other religions can receive divine grace, it is also certain that objectively speaking they are in a gravely deficient situation in comparison with those who, in the Church, have the fullness of the means of salvation" (no. 21).

The document is rightly called a "Declaration." This is not the voice of a listening church authority. The Asian bishops must know now if they did not know before that synods in Rome have become a farce. The Vatican is not interested in hearing the voices of local churches. The Vatican's interest is in promoting a narrow understanding of "salvation" that supports the Vatican's claim to unique spiritual authority in the world.

Limiting our understanding of salvation to what this document "declares" must be firmly held takes us back into scriptural literalism, an interventionist God, severe limitation on the presence and activity of God's Spirit, and exclusive claims to religious "truth." Fidelity to this approach, it seems, will ensure that none of us are misled by "listening to the voice of God ... in the voice of the times."

We have to push on beyond the disappointing teaching of this declaration if our Christian faith is to mature, and one way to do this is to be more catholic in our understanding of "salvation."

We can be more catholic if we clearly separate our understanding of God's work of "salvation" and Jesus' role in this from dependency on an actual fall that caused a disruption of God's presence and friendship with us, on the belief that Jesus "as an innocent lamb merited life for us by his blood which he freely shed," on the belief that the activity of God's Spirit in our world is dependent on the Son of God "descending and ascending" and only then granting the life-giving, healing presence of God's Spirit to humankind.

A more catholic and more believable understanding of salvation will take as its starting point that God's Spirit has always been present in the slow development of life on this planet. In this perspective salvation will not be understood as winning back something that was lost but rather the movement of God's Spirit within human cultures to deepen awareness of connectedness with the Transcendent, to move men and women to greater depths of co-operation and care and generosity, to assure men and women of hope and healing in the face of inevitable pain and tragedy in this fragile world, and to move all of us to live human life as best we can, in ways that ennoble and dignify ourselves and our neighbors.

This process of salvation began long, long before Jesus, and its fruits are to be seen in any person who at any time and in any place lived what we would call in ordinary language "a thoroughly good and decent human life." The process worked in individual lives and it worked also in cultures and in religious movements working for the betterment of humankind.

A genuinely catholic approach to salvation would have us stand shoulder to shoulder with anyone, anywhere in this human quest—as the Asian bishops are trying to do in their culture—and in this shared concern we Christians could share how the teaching and the life and death of Jesus reveal to us Christians the way God's Spirit works in human lives and how we, because of this man, have been "set free" from fear and superstition, know we are loved intimately by God, and know we are entrusted with the responsibility of making God's "reign" visible in human society.

A truly catholic theology of salvation today would anchor itself in the story of Jesus and in the belief that all people at all times have been and are God's people. It would proclaim its belief in God revealed in all of creation and in all people at all times. It would manifest enormous appreciation and respect for diversity since this is clearly the pattern of God's revelation. It would be missionary, not in the sense of taking a deposit of faith to many places, but in shaping religious imagination and thinking for these times and in breaking new ground in religious dialogue.

This "catholic" theology would be big-minded and big-hearted, expansive, adaptable, generous in its breadth of vision and humble in its acceptance that God is not definable in human language.

This "catholic" theology would avoid interpreting the story of Jesus in a framework that sets Christianity above, against, apart from, or better than any other way God has been or is being revealed on earth. Jesus' teaching concerning the reign of God in our midst is clearly counter to such a theological framework. The reign of God is present in every good and decent human action and endeavor. It is the universality of this presence that should shape "catholic" thinking and practice. It is at the heart of the good news Christianity has learned from Jesus and wants to share with all people.

The task of shaping a "catholic" theology is the Pentecost challenge of our times. The New Story provides a wonderful context and opportunity for this genuine "catholic" theology. One of its major assets is that it provides for the first time in human history a common story, accessible to people of all cultures and all religions. It is an awesome story about the beginning and growth of the universe, the formation of galaxies, stars, and planets. The story leads us to contemplate our planet and the precious gift of life here with a renewed sense of appreciation and wonder.

Time and space take on new dimensions for everyone exposed to this story. Figures dealing with size and space are beyond our comprehension. We hear that a thimble full of matter from a neutron star would weigh one hundred million tons. We marvel and shake our heads in wonder when we learn that our sun, one of billions of stars in this galaxy, converts six hundred million tons of hydrogen into helium every second and has been doing so for more than four billion years. Every hour the universe expands another billion miles. And we learn that every atom in our bodies was present in a star billions of years ago.

There are still many gaps in the New Story and much scientific discussion and disagreement on particular issues, but overall we have a story to enchant and delight the whole world. Here, in this story, we must surely stand today and ask the questions that are common to people of all times and places. Is there an intelligent Supreme Being? If so, what is the nature of this Being and how is creation connected with this Being? In particular, what is the relationship of humankind with this Being? Who are we? Is there existence beyond death?

Science will not give us answers to these questions and we should not expect it to. We are dealing with mystery, the unknown, the realm of faith. We are dealing with questions concerning the ultimate meaning of human existence, trying to make sense of who we are as we contemplate the universe, the world, and the societies in which we live.

We Christians believe that the life and teaching of Jesus of Nazareth are a "light" for us as we engage these questions. The story of Jesus helps us articulate a faith understanding of human existence that sets us free from fear of the unknown and affirms a wonderful connectedness with the Being we call "God."

The Jesus story can be told with a renewed enthusiasm today. Joined with the New Story, the story of Jesus has an even greater capacity to delight and uplift us because it tells us anew of God's Spirit at work in the wonder of creation and in the wonder of who we are. This is a story "in keeping with the whole," a story worth telling over and over again.

Discussion Points

1. What difference does a contemporary understanding of the universe and the development of life on earth make to the way the story of Jesus is to be told and understood?

2. What could be the practical implications of adopting a truly "catholic" theology at a local level?

Recommended Reading

Armstrong, Karen. *A History of God*. New York: Ballantine Books, 1993.

Berry, Thomas. *The Dream of the Earth*. San Francisco: Sierra Club Books, 1988.

Birch, Charles. *A Purpose for Everything: Religion in a Postmodern Worldview*. Mystic, Conn.: Twenty-Third Publications, 1990.Originally published as *On Purpose*. Sydney: New South Wales University Press, 1990.

Dunn, James D. G. *Christology in the Making: A New Testament Inquiry into the Origins of the Doctrine of the Incarnation*. London: SCM Press, 1989, and Grand Rapids, Mich.: Eerdmans, 1996.

Edwards, Denis. *The God of Evolution: A Trinitarian Theology*. New York: Paulist Press, 1999.

Guthridge, Ian. *The Rise and Decline of the Christian Empire*. Middle Park, Victoria, Australia: Medici School/Publications, 1999.

Johnson, Elizabeth A. *She Who Is: The Mystery of God in Feminist Theological Discourse*. New York: Crossroad, 1994.

————. *Consider Jesus: Waves of Renewal in Christology*. New York: Crossroad, 1996.

Lonergan, Anne, and Caroline Richards, eds. *Thomas Berry and the New Cosmology*. Mystic, Conn.: Twenty-Third Publications, 1991.

Murphy, Desmond. *A Return to Spirit: After the Mythic Church*. New York: Crossroad, and Alexandria, New South Wales: E. J. Dwyer, 1997.

Nolan, Albert. *Jesus before Christianity*. Maryknoll, N.Y.: Orbis Books, 1978.

O'Murchu, Diarmuid. *Quantum Theology: Spiritual Implications of the New Physics*. New York: Crossroad, 1997.

Rubenstein, Richard. *When Jesus Became God: The Struggle to Define Christianity during the Last Days of Rome*. San Diego: Harcourt, 2000.

Segundo, Juan Luis. *The Liberation of Dogma: Faith, Revelation and Dogmatic Teaching Authority*. Maryknoll, N.Y.: Orbis Books, 1992.

Spong, John Shelby. *Why Christianity Must Change or Die: A Bishop Speaks to Believers in Exile*. San Francisco: HarperSanFrancisco, 1998.

Swimme, Brian. *The Universe Is a Green Dragon: A Cosmic Creation Story*. Santa Fe, N.Mex.: Bear & Company, 1984.

———. *The Hidden Heart of the Cosmos: Humanity and the New Story*. Maryknoll, N.Y.: Orbis Books, 1996.

Swimme, Brian, and Thomas Berry. *The Universe Story: A Celebration of the Unfolding of the Cosmos*. San Francisco: HarperSanFrancisco, and London: Penguin Books, 1992.

Wilber, Ken. *The Marriage of Sense and Soul: Integrating Science and Religion*. New York: Random House, and Melbourne: Hill of Content, 1998.